Please remember that this is a library book,
and that it belongs only temporarily to each
person who uses it. Be considerate. Do
not write in this, or any, library book.

D1412174

EEC ISBN 0-931629-19-5
NEA ISBN 0-8106-1881-8

Cover and book design by Rappy & Company, Inc.

Printed by Scott Printing Corporation.

Printing history:
First printing, September 1998
Second printing, December 2000

The drawings in this Guide were created by children from the Cabot Elementary School in Newton, Massachusetts and the Manhattan Country Day School in New York City. The quotes are from teachers at Cabot Elementary School and Manhattan Country Day School who participated in the pilot testing of the Guide.

Funding was received from the Women's Educational Equity Act Program and the Safe and Drug Free Schools and Communities Act of the United States Department of Education. Additional funding was received from The Aaron Diamond Foundation and the Ms. Foundation for Education and Communication.

The contents of this Guide were developed under a grant from the Department of Education. However, these contents do not necessarily represent the policy of the Department of Education, and you should not assume endorsement by the Federal Government.

The opinions expressed in this book should not be construed as representing the policy or position of the National Education Association. Materials published by the NEA Professional Library are intended to be discussion documents for educators who are concerned with specialized interests of the profession.

Library of Congress Cataloging-in-Publication Data

Froschl, Merle.
   Quit it! : a teacher's guide on teasing and bullying for use with students in grades K-3 / written by Merle Froschl, Barbara Sprung, Nancy Mullin-Rindler with Nan Stein and Nancy Gropper.
      p. cm.
   Includes bibliographical references (p.).
   ISBN 0-931629-19-5 (EEC). — ISBN 0-8106-1881-8 (NEA)
   1. School discipline. 2. Bullying—Prevention. 3. Education, Primary—Activity programs. I. Sprung, Barbara. II. Mullin-Rindler, Nancy, 1951- III. Title.
LB3012.F77 1998   98-8135
372.1102'4—dc21   CIP

A Teacher's Guide on Teasing and Bullying for Use with Students in Grades K-3

WRITTEN BY

Merle Froschl

Barbara Sprung

Nancy Mullin-Rindler

with Nan Stein and Nancy Gropper

Educational Equity Concepts, Inc.
New York, New York

Wellesley College Center for Research on Women
Wellesley, Massachusetts

NEA Professional Library
National Education Association
Washington, DC

1998

Table of Contents

Acknowledgments

It is our pleasure to express our appreciation to the many people who helped us during the development, research, and pilot testing phases of the work that led to the publication of *Quit it! A Teacher's Guide on Teasing and Bullying for Use with Students in Grades K-3.*

Beginning with the development phase, we wish to thank Michelle Fine, Professor of Psychology, Graduate Center, City University of New York, for her wisdom and knowledge. We also extend our thanks to graduate students Corrine Bertram and Maya Poran, who conducted the extensive literature search that informed our work.

For their participation during the research phase in New York City, we express our appreciation to Jim Mazza, Superintendent of Community School District 3; Roberta Kirshbaum, Principal of P.S. 75; and to the teachers, parents, and children who were part of the research study.

In Massachusetts, for their help and participation during the research phase, we'd like to thank Marge Sauer, Director of Curriculum and Staff Development of the Framingham School Department. We are also grateful to the principals, teachers, children, and parents of the Miriam F. McCarthy, Potter Road, and Mary E. Stapleton elementary schools in Framingham who welcomed us and shared their thoughts, concerns, feelings, and personal experiences as we researched teasing and bullying.

We could not have done this work without our dedicated and knowledgeable research assistants. In New York City, Jennifer Pastor and Lynn Rose Walker. In Massachusetts, Alina Martinez, Debra Olshever, and Barb Wilder-Smith – many thanks for their experienced observation skills, sensitivity, and valuable insights.

For helping us pilot the Guide, in Massachusetts, we are indebted to Marilynne Quarcoo, Principal of the Cabot Elementary School in Newton, for her interest and support of this project; and to the dedicated Cabot teachers who gave much more of their time than we asked and whose openness, willingness to experiment, thoughtful comments, and wealth of ideas helped shape this Guide: Penny Benjamin, Lynda Cain, Kelli Canniff, Patti Dukakis, Jodi Escalante, Nancy ("Sue") MacFarland, Marcie Mann, Matt Miller, Melissa Ramgren, and Lois Strother. Thanks also go to the hundreds of Cabot students for their interest, honesty, enthusiasm, and great ideas about ways to stop teasing and bullying – this is for you!

We'd like to thank Terry Meier, Associate Professor of Education at Wheelock College, for sharing her ideas and listing of multicultural books with us. We 'd also like to thank Julia Rindler and many of her friends for letting us pick their brains about books they like, what they think and do about teasing and bullying, and for their patience and good humor as they endured lots of "Well, what if…" questions.

In New York City, the administrators and teachers at the Manhattan Country School also gave of themselves well beyond what we asked of them during the pilot testing of the Guide. They added ideas, activities, and worksheets; they collected children's work; and they gave us invaluable feedback in written form and verbally in several late afternoon meetings. We express our appreciation to Michèle Solá, Director; Lois Gelernt, Lower School Director; and to the teachers – Doris Finkel, Sarah Leibowits, Sandra Lim, Nadjwa Norton, Krina Patel, Shobana Ram, and Toni-Leigh Savage. We thank the students, from whom we learned so much. We couldn't have done it without you!

We extend our appreciation to Annie Ellman, Executive Director of the Center for Anti-Violence Education; and to Kristin Mullins, Senior Instructor, Children's Empowerment Project at the Center. We had the privilege of watching them work with young children, building their self-confidence and cooperative skills through wonderful, non-competitive activities. They let us adapt some of those activities for this Guide, and they provided insightful feedback on what we had done.

Finally, we thank Floyd Rappy, of Rappy & Company Inc., for his patience, good will, and talented graphic design.

Introduction

Classroom bullying is more prevalent than many educators think, and experts say it should no longer be tolerated as "part of growing up." (*Education Week*, May 28, 1997, p. 19)

Most Americans do not take bullying very seriously – not even school personnel, a surprising finding given that most bullying takes place in schools. If Americans think at all about it, they tend to think that bullying is a given of childhood, at most a passing stage, one inhabited largely by boys who will, simply, inevitably, be boys. (*Psychology Today*, September/October 1995, p. 52)

IT'S ELEMENTARY

Unfortunately, teasing and bullying are facts of life for young students. Ask any elementary school teacher, and she or he will tell you that this kind of behavior is a daily occurrence that disrupts teaching and learning.

We all would agree that school should be a safe place for students – a place where they are welcome, comfortable, and free to learn. But researchers have documented that it is precisely at school where bullying takes place most frequently. And, in school, bullying occurs most often where there is little or no adult supervision – hallways, playground, lunchroom, gym, and bathrooms.

Recent research conducted by Educational Equity Concepts and the Wellesley College Center for Research on Women found that teasing and bullying are a part of the fabric of daily life for students in kindergarten through grade three. Findings of our year-long study, which included classroom observations, interviews with children, and focus groups with teachers and parents, parallel those of other formal research studies that have been conducted both within and outside the United States:

- Teasing and bullying are frequent occurrences in elementary school classrooms;
- Boys initiate most of the teasing and bullying incidents, but both girls and boys are the recipients;
- Boys are more likely to respond physically, while girls are more likely to respond verbally to incidents initiated against them;

- Teachers and other adults frequently do not intervene – their predominant response is to remain uninvolved;
- Students feel that adults do not pay attention or support them in ways that resolve the teasing and bullying;
- Students want adults to become more involved.

During focus group sessions, teachers identified teasing and bullying as tremendous problems that negatively affect their classrooms and their ability to teach. They discussed the fact that, in addition to gender, any perceived differences among students can serve as a trigger for teasing and bullying, including race, ethnicity, class, age, and physical differences. While teachers felt that early intervention is important, they also stated that teasing and bullying are not topics that are typically included as an integral part of the early elementary school curriculum.

Quit it! A Teacher's Guide on Teasing and Bullying for Use with Students in Grades K-3 was written to address these concerns and to provide teachers in grades K-3 with a proactive, gender-sensitive approach to addressing teasing and bullying.

DEFINING THE TERMS

Dan Olweus, a professor of psychology at the University of Bergen in Norway, has researched bullying for more than 20 years. He defines bullying in this way: "A student is being bullied or victimized when he or she is exposed, repeatedly and over time, to negative actions on the part of one or more other students."[1]

He explains that "negative actions" can be carried out by words, by physical contact, or in other ways, such as making faces, gesturing, or intentional exclusion from a group. While Olweus' definition emphasizes negative actions that are carried out repeatedly and over time, he and other researchers feel that students also can be harmed by occasional incidents of bullying.

Is teasing different from bullying? In our opinion, only as a matter of degree. Teasing can be a form of banter or humor, but that is not what is being addressed in this Guide. We're concerned with teasing and bullying as a continuum of intentionally hurtful behavior. On one end there might be mildly annoying behavior, which almost any child might dismiss. Further along the line, there might be disparaging language, taking someone's possessions or insulting a family member. Still further along, teasing may become bullying as defined above, involving abusive language, physical contact, or intentional exclusion.

THE NEED FOR A FOCUS ON GENDER

All students – girls and boys – can find themselves the targets of bullies and can themselves initiate the teasing and bullying. It has been found that typically boys are more frequently victims of physical bullying while girls experience more exclusion. The fact is, however, that while both girls and boys are the targets, boys do most (though not all) of the teasing and bullying. In our research study, we observed boys initiating three times as many incidents as girls. However, it is important to keep in mind that this is not an indication that "boys are bad," but rather that we all must do a much better job of addressing aggressive behavior in young boys to counteract the prevailing messages they receive from the media and society in general.

Girls and boys are bombarded with messages about sex roles from birth. Young children learn about how girls and boys are "supposed" to behave through a variety of factors. Toys, games, stories, clothing, room furnishings, and adult's responses all play a part. Boy's clothing, even in infancy, reflects sports motifs; their playthings are often toy weapons; their riding toys replicate motorcycles – just to name a few examples. Girls, on the other hand, are most often surrounded from infancy by soft colors, soft toys, and domestic playthings.

Research has shown that boy babies are allowed to roam further from their mothers or caregivers while girls are kept at much closer range. In other studies, researchers have dressed the same infant in typical girl or boy clothes. When dressed as a girl, adults describe the infant using words like "delicate," "sweet," and "tiny." When the infant is dressed in "boy" clothes, the descriptive words are "strong," "big," "a bruiser." So adult expectations play a strong role in helping to shape how boys and girls view the world and their role in it.

Typically, expectations for girls and boys are quite different. Girls are encouraged to act nurturing and to be emotionally expressive; adults are protective when girls stretch their boundaries; and risk-taking is often discouraged. In many instances, aggression in girls is deemed "unladylike" and strongly discouraged. Girls are taught, subtly or unconsciously, that they need to be protected rather than to stand up for themselves.

Again subtly, or even unconsciously, boys are often encouraged to act physically or aggressively. They are expected to be dominant, rewarded when they are adventurous, and their risk-taking behavior is considered natural for their sex. Then, when boys act like they think boys should act – sometimes pushing, pinching, calling names, and yes, kissing girls – adults tend to either ignore the intimidating behavior, saying "boys will be boys," or overreact and label boys sexual harassers, as in incidents reported in the press.

We do not think that sexual harassment is an appropriate term to use with young students. But behavior such as sexual harassment does not spring up abruptly in adolescence or adulthood. If teasing and bullying behavior is not addressed in the early grades, boys and girls both may learn that boys are likely to get away with abusive behavior. The antecedents of peer-to-peer sexual harassment in schools may very well be found in teasing and bullying in the early grades.

Bernard Lefkowitz, author of *Our Guys*, a book about the rape of a 17-year-old retarded young woman by four of Glen Ridge, New Jersey's most popular athletes, theorizes that this horrific abuse could not have taken place had it not been for the community's long-standing tolerance of aggressive behaviors and indifference to how girls were treated by boys. He writes:

While as children, girls expected to be accepted as equal human beings by the boys they knew....[In time they] learned they had to submit to whatever the boys asked of them, and, as time passed, the boys kept asking for more. Suppose the girls refused to submit. Who could they go to for support?... Who would stand up for these young women? Who would say to these boys, 'This is wrong. Stop it.'?... The message was clear: Guys had unchallenged power. ... Because adults did not intervene to stop the abuse, many girls questioned their own worth, not only to boys but also to adults whose judgment really counted. ... [Adults] could have provided an alternative model of behavior to youngsters, one that emphasized fairness, compassion, humanity, and decency.[2]

YOU MAKE A DIFFERENCE

As teachers, it is important to provide alternative models of behavior for boys and girls. However, research confirms that teachers most often do not intervene when they witness incidents of teasing and bullying. Teachers and other adults were uninvolved or ignored 71% of the observed incidents of teasing and bullying in our research study. When teachers do not respond, whether out of frustration or a desire to let students "work it out for themselves," students perceive the absence of teacher response or involvement as tacit acceptance of aggressive or bullying behavior. Since boys are the predominant initiators of these incidents, students may also see teachers' lack of response as giving boys license to behave in these ways. Thus, students learn a great deal about "acceptable" gender roles in school settings and beyond.

The good news is that you can make a big difference. The attitudes and behavior of teachers are decisive factors in preventing teasing and bullying behaviors, as well as in redirecting such behaviors into more positive actions. We know that creating a classroom learning environment that fosters respect for difference and avoids gender stereotyping sets a tone that affects how students behave and treat each other. The way adults interact with students also directly affects students' behavior. In addition, classroom rules and routines help students respond more positively and help them understand the connection between their actions and the consequences when rules are applied fairly but not rigidly.

ACTION BEGINS WITH AWARENESS

Adults in the school community (teachers, staff, administrators, and parents) need to become aware of the importance of taking teasing and bullying seriously, and they must commit themselves to doing something about it. By using *Quit it!*, you are taking positive action in that direction. In order to

reduce teasing and bullying behavior, both adults and students need to work together to create a safe and welcoming learning environment that fosters self-respect and respect for others. Some general pointers include:

- Intervene with students when an incident occurs. Be sure to include *all* participants in the incident: the initiators, recipients, *and* bystanders. Students who stand by while someone else is being bullied feel vulnerable that they might be next, and powerless if they do nothing to help.

- Integrate discussions and activities about teasing and bullying into your teaching. This enables you to address the issue in an ongoing way, not just when an incident occurs.

- Provide help for students to develop skills in empathy, problem-solving, and anger management.

- Create opportunities for cooperative learning, both in your classroom and, whenever possible, across grades. Many schools have cross-grade "buddies" for reading or other subject areas. These promote better understanding and acceptance among students and may reduce the incidence of "big kids" picking on "little kids."

- Provide opportunities for boys and girls to work together. Avoid segregating students by gender for lines, seating, teams, etc.

A SCHOOL-WIDE APPROACH

Of course, you can't do it alone. Support from the school's administration is essential. A clearly-stated, consistent school-wide policy, distributed to everyone in the school community, has been shown to be an effective tool in combatting teasing and bullying. The administration can be particularly helpful with regard to supervision during recess and lunch, times when teasing and bullying can get out of hand. Last, but not least, involving parents is a critical element in reducing teasing and bullying. Communicate with parents about what you are doing in your classroom to address teasing and bullying; hold parent workshops on the topic; and provide suggestions to help parents talk with their children on the topic.

THEY HAVE TO BE TAUGHT

Beginning early is the key. Just as the building blocks for later learning exist in the early elementary classroom, so do the seeds for later behavior, attitudes, and adult interactions.

In the 1950s, South Pacific, the landmark musical play by Rogers and Hart which dealt with racial prejudice, included a song sung by young Pacific Island children in the cast. It's title was, "You Have To Be Taught," and the first line stated, "You have to be taught to hate and fear." This sentiment was repeated in November 1997 at a White House Conference on Hate Crimes:

Children have to be taught to hate. And as they come more and more of age and they get into more and more environments where they can be taught that, we need to make sure that someone is teaching them not to do so. The most important thing we can do is to reach these kids while they're young enough to learn.

Children learn to read the true arrangement of power in society by watching how adults around them act and resolve problems. They learn whether the principles of fairness and equality are meant to apply to them, or not. They learn whether these principles apply equally to all people. They learn whether we value those who stand up against injustice. It is up to us, their teachers, parents, and other family members, to help them learn well.

Because the issue of teasing and bullying, with its subtle but strong gender subtext, is a reality of classroom life in elementary school, *Quit it!* is intended to provide you with a valuable tool for addressing the issues in proactive ways. It is our hope that this Guide will help you create a welcoming, comfortable, and safe learning environment for all your students, regardless of their gender, race, ethnicity, disability, class or any other individual difference that might make them the target of teasing and bullying.

---

1. D. Olweus, *Bullying At School: What We Know and What We Can Do* (Oxford, UK: Blackwell, 1993), p.9.

2. B. Lefkowitz, *Our Guys: The Glen Ridge Rape and the Secret Life of the Perfect Suburb* (Berkeley: University of California Press, 1997), pp. 422-424.

NOTE: See "References: For Further Reading," a listing of books and articles on research related to the issues discussed in this Introduction, and "History of the Project," a description of the research conducted by Educational Equity Concepts and the Wellesley College Center for Research on Women.

How To Use This Guide

Thematic Structure

Quit it! A Teacher's Guide on Teasing and Bullying for Use with Students in Grades K-3 is divided into three major themes. The themes are arranged sequentially, and we suggest that you start with Creating Our Rules early in the school year and proceed to Talking about Teasing and Bullying and Exploring Courage in turn.

THEME ONE – Creating Our Rules
Students discuss and define the meaning of a rule; they think about how rules help us get along and what happens when there are no rules. Students write rules for their classroom and revisit them throughout the school year; they look at rules in the larger context of the school and community; and they exercise their imaginations and dreams through writing about an ideal world.

THEME TWO – Talking about Teasing and Bullying
Teasing and bullying become topics for ongoing discussion in the classroom. Students explore what makes them feel welcome and unwelcome in school and identify areas of the classroom and school where they feel safe and unsafe. They talk about what it feels like to be angry and express a variety of feelings through body language as well as words. They also practice ways of responding to teasing and bullying situations in realistic and safe ways.

THEME THREE – Exploring Courage
Students define courage as it relates to teasing and bullying. They learn that this kind of courage does not involve undue risk-taking, violence, or weaponry. They explore ways to "do the right thing" and to "listen to their strong side," to stand up to injustice, to resist peer pressure, and not to be a bystander in instances of teasing and bullying. They analyze how barriers and exclusion keep people apart and cause hurt, and they explore how courage and friendship interconnect.

Each theme contains the following elements:

- A list of *Goals* followed by a *Students Will Learn* section describing the learning objectives and the concepts that are conveyed to students.

- *Background* providing a brief discussion about the topic and how it relates to teasing and bullying.

- *Sequential Lessons* carrying out the main ideas of the themes, and including *Activities* appropriate for grades K-1, 1-2, and 2-3.

- *Problem-Solving* including scenarios to act out using puppets and role-plays, stop-action stories, and vignettes.

- *Literature Connection* providing information about related picture and chapter books, which can be used as classroom or homework reading.

- *Connecting with Families* including ways for communicating ideas from the lessons with parents, as well as a letter that can be reproduced and sent home suggesting ways for parents to continue the discussion with their children.

The Activities

Within each lesson there is at least one activity for use with students either in Grades K-1, 1-2, or 2-3. Some activities indicate that they can work successfully over several grade spans. While the grade indications have been included to help you select the activities most appropriate for your students, we urge you to keep an open mind as you read through the Guide. During the pilot testing, we saw that many of the more complex activities were adapted successfully for younger students and, conversely, many of the simpler activities were expanded to a higher level of discussion by older students.

Each activity contains *Materials/Preparation Needed* and *step-by-step instructions*. When children's literature is listed in Materials, the approximate grade level and type of book appear in parentheses following the name of the book. If the activity has a related *worksheet*, it will be found at the end of the lesson in which the activity appears. The worksheets have been designed to be easily reproduced. Throughout the activities there are *Teacher Tips* and *Anecdotes*, which are ideas that came from teachers who pilot tested the Guide. *Student Work* (writing and drawing) from the pilot also is included. *Notes* are used to focus attention on alternative ways to approach the activity.

If *Quit it!* is being used at various grade levels within your school and, as a result, your students have experienced some of the activities before they enter your class, you can begin the theme with one of the more complex activities. Also, keep in mind that all of the ideas bear repeating and, as students mature, they will bring a different level of consciousness, understanding, and experience to the issues.

Integrated Skill-Building

The activities in *Quit it!*, while focusing on teasing and bullying, are purposely designed to promote skill-building across many subject areas: language arts (through reading and writing), math (through charting and graphing), social studies (through learning about community and social justice), and physical education (through movement and relaxation). This design allows both the activities and the topics of teasing and bullying to be integrated into the daily life of the classroom.

The activities employ developmentally-appropriate strategies that are familiar to teachers in the early primary grades: story time, reading, group discussions, experience charts, drawings, art projects, creative story writing, journal writing, role-playing, puppet plays, charting, and graphing. Through the activities, students learn to become critical thinkers as they negotiate their relationships with others, observe the world around them, and develop their sense of fair play.

Auxiliary Sections

In addition to the themes, *Quit it!* includes three auxiliary sections:

PHYSICAL GAMES AND EXERCISES
This section includes ideas for movement games that promote inclusion and cooperation rather than competition, and techniques for relaxation, calming, stress reduction, and letting off steam. They are meant to be used informally and as needed during the school day so that students, individually and in groups, can engage in moving, stretching, and breathing activities.

PROBLEM-SOLVING TECHNIQUES

This section describes a variety of approaches to help students work through solutions for teasing and bullying situations. Included are effective ways to use books, puppets, role-plays, stop-action stories, and vignettes. Sample problem-solving scenarios and vignettes are included within each theme; suggestions for developing your own scenarios are included in this section.

ANNOTATED BIBLIOGRAPHY

This comprehensive listing includes picture and chapter books for students, and readings and resource materials for teachers and parents. Each of the books for students indicates the appropriate grade levels and is coded according to the related theme(s). Also included are suggestions for selecting and screening books for students, beyond those suggested in the Guide.

Conclusion

Teasing and bullying are pervasive problems in the lives of elementary students in schools across the country. The problem will not go away after one discussion. In addition, students need support and practice to respond successfully to teasing and bullying situations. Therefore, *Quit it!* is designed to be used in an ongoing way. The topic needs to be revisited, using a variety of different activities, techniques, and approaches, throughout the school year *and* from year to year as well.

If *Quit it!* is being used by other teachers in your school, we suggest that you form a teacher discussion group to talk about how it's going and to share ideas and strategies. Finally, we encourage you to use this Guide as a catalyst to expand upon your own lessons to make the topics of teasing and bullying an integral part of the teaching and learning in your classroom.

Creating Our Rules

Rules keep people safe and feeling comfortable.

– Third-grade student

We have been constantly talking about rules in the classroom and why they're important. This is the students' first year in school, so it is always relevant and in need of being discussed.

— Kindergarten teacher

In This Theme

LESSON ONE: WHAT IS A RULE?

K-3 Activity: The Story of Ridley —
  A Place with No Rules
K-3 Activity: Making rules for Ridley
1-2 Activity: Writing a definition
2-3 Activity: Creative story writing/illustrating

LESSON TWO: CREATING RULES FOR THE CLASSROOM

K-3 Activity: Brainstorming and writing rules
1-2 Activity: Creating a rules quilt

LESSON THREE: RULES OUTSIDE THE CLASSROOM

K-1 Activity: Rules for a friendly playground
1-2 Activity: All-school rules poster project
1-2 Activity: Connecting home/school/
  community rules
2-3 Activity: Writing about an ideal world

PROBLEM SOLVING

K-3 Activity: Telling not tattling
  *Vignettes: Meg and Peter, The Cookies,
  The Insult, Pam's Problem, Breaking a Rule,
  The 4-Square Game*

LITERATURE CONNECTIONS

CONNECTING WITH FAMILIES

  Take-home: Family Activity Letter

Goals

- To help students understand the reasons for rules of social behavior
- To engage students in the process of creating classroom rules that foster civil behavior
- To create a climate of safety, comfort, and cooperation in the classroom/school
- To help foster positive relationships between girls and boys
- To create rules that alleviate situations leading to teasing and bullying behavior
- To establish that teasing and bullying behavior will not be tolerated
- To convey consequences of teasing and bullying behavior

Students Will Learn

- That they have decision-making abilities
- That they have a stake in creating civil behavior — boys and girls respecting each other, boys respecting other boys, girls respecting other girls, students respecting adults, and adults respecting students
- That rules are important for their safety and comfort, and that students are expected to follow them
- That breaking rules brings consequences
- That teasing and bullying are against the rules

Background

Whether or not children have been in child care or preschool settings, kindergarten is a major transition in terms of negotiating relationships, group dynamics, and school culture. For some students, kindergarten is a first experience for group social interactions outside their extended families.

From the time they enter school, students are expected to conform to many different kinds of rules — classroom rules, lunchroom rules, hallway rules, playground rules, bathroom rules. These rules may be quite different from those a child has learned at home or in other settings. School rules are constructed with positive intentions by adults, and teachers usually spend time at the beginning of each school year introducing rules about safety, school and classroom governance, taking turns, and promoting civility among students.

The "whys" for having rules, however, are usually not part of the discussion teachers have with students. Discussing the reasons behind rules helps students understand how rules support civil behavior, personal responsibility, empathy, and a sense of community. Without this understanding, students may abuse the rules as a tattling device or use them to wield power over others in ways that may lead to teasing and bullying behavior.

By second and third grade, students become especially concerned about the notion of fairness. For this reason, rules and how students conduct themselves are often at the center of arguments — especially when playing games. These arguments can lead to teasing, physical bullying, and bullying in the form of exclusion. As a matter of course, or as situations arise, you can use these situations as an opportunity to discuss rules (e.g., How are the rules of the games decided on? How can you change the rules?); the role of gender (e.g., Do boys and girls have different rules for the same game?); and concepts such as fair play (e.g., Are some people treated differently? How do you decide who can play?).

The activities that follow are designed to involve students in "rule-making" with a focus on how rules help us to get along, particularly with regard to teasing and bullying, and the relationships between girls and boys. The making of rules is more effective when it is part of a group process in which everyone is involved. If possible, the activities should be carried out at the beginning of the school year, so everyone starts out together invested in creating an environment that reinforces kind behavior. But rethinking and revising existing rules can (and should) occur throughout the year.

LESSON ONE: WHAT IS A RULE?
Students arrive at the meaning of a rule.

K-3 Activity: The Story of Ridley — A Place with No Rules
(1-2 class sessions)

MATERIALS NEEDED: Chart paper; markers; "The Story of Ridley" [If students have already heard and discussed "Ridley," extend the discussion by reading selections from *The Butter Battle* (1-3, picture), *Jumanji* (1-3, picture), *Alice's Adventures in Wonderland* (2-3, chapter), or the *Wizard of Oz* (3, chapter), books that highlight how rules can be arbitrary and confusing; see Annotated Bibliography]

1. Ask students, "What is a rule?"

2. Make a list of all the rules students know about on chart paper. These can be rules at home (picking up toys and putting them away); at school (raising hand to ask question during class meeting); or in the community (putting litter in the litter basket).

3. Once students have thought about the rules they know, ask them:

Why do you think we have rules?
What do you think might happen if there were no rules?
What do you think might happen if we had no rules for getting along with each other or playing together?

➤ **TEACHER TIP:**

Keep the chart of rules the students come up with. You can refer to it to identify common themes and ideas as students arrive at their own definition of a rule in a later activity.

4. Introduce "Ridley" by telling students you are going to read them a story about a very unusual place — a place with no rules. Ask them, "Do you think you would like to live in this type of place? Let's see..."

➤ **TEACHER TIP:**

"The Story of Ridley" can be read all the way through, or you can make it more interactive by stopping in appropriate places and asking students, "What do you think happened?" The places where students can "fill in" the story are marked in parentheses with a suggestion about what might happen.

THE STORY OF RIDLEY — A PLACE WITH NO RULES

Once, a very long time ago, there was a place called Ridley where there were no rules. There were grownups and children in this place and there were animals, too, like cows, goats, pigs, and geese.

Because there were no rules, sometimes the animals came into the houses. Once a pig sat on a baby (and the baby got hurt). Once a goose wandered into the house (and pecked all the stuffing out of a chair).

And the children were always getting into danger, because there were no safety rules. One boy went too near the stove (and burned his hand). One girl ran across the street without looking (and she ran into a goat).

Children and grownups didn't brush their teeth (and everyone had cavities and toothaches). Grownups worked whenever they felt like it, so many chores were never done. The garbage piled up (and people got sick from the germs).

Children in Ridley didn't learn very much because there were no rules about attending school. Sometimes children came to class because they liked to learn, but there were no teachers. Sometimes teachers came because they liked to teach, but no children were there to learn.

Because there were no rules about being polite or kind, grownups and children were often mean to each other. Some people in Ridley teased and bullied others all the time. Girls and boys were always fighting with each other.

Ridley was a mess of a place. No one living there was very happy. Something had to be done.

5. Tell students that you will be discussing "Ridley" again. Ask them to think about rules that would help Ridley become a better place to live.

K-3 Activity: Making rules for Ridley (1 class session)

MATERIALS NEEDED: Index cards or paper (for pairs); chart paper; markers

1. Briefly review "Ridley."

2. Ask students, "What do you think it would be like to live in a place like Ridley?"

➤ **TEACHER TIP:**

> During discussion, students probably will begin by focussing on the more concrete aspects of the story — animals in houses, garbage in street. Allow them to explore these ideas, but bring them back to the "people issues" — especially boys and girls teasing and bullying and being mean to each other.

3. Suggest that the class make up a set of rules for Ridley. Talk about categories of rules needed, e.g. safety, health, civil behavior. Younger students can work on the rules as a class. Older students can work in pairs on rules for the different categories. In the civil behavior category, have students think about rules to help girls and boys who live in Ridley get along without teasing, bullying, and fighting with each other.

4. If you do the activity in pairs, have each pair read the rules that they came up with to the class and record them on chart paper. Or, if done as a class discussion, list the rules directly on chart paper.

5. Ask students if they think any rules Ridley needs are still missing and, if so, add them to the chart.

• •

NOTE: *If you have chosen one of the other books suggested for this activity, create a set of rules* *that are fair rather than confusing or arbitrary.*

• •

1-2 Activity: Writing a definition (1 class session)

MATERIALS NEEDED: Writing paper; pencils; chart paper; markers

1. Have students work in pairs or small groups to write a definition of a rule.

➤ **TEACHER TIP:**

> If students are not familiar with the concept of a definition, have them first look up some different, but familiar, words in the dictionary.

CREATING OUR RULES | 15

2. Have each pair or small group share their definition with the whole class.

3. After all the groups have read their definition, have the class come up with an agreed-upon definition. Point out that the definition can have several parts. For example:

> "A rule is something we follow that tells us how to act. Some rules are written to keep us safe. Other rules help people be kind to each other."

2-3 Activity: Creative story writing/illustrating (1 class session)

MATERIALS NEEDED: Paper; pencils; crayons or markers

1. As a cooperative small-group activity, ask students to create their own stories about a place with no rules. Give students an opening line, for example:

> Long ago in the land of (be sure to let students come up with their own name),
> there was a place (or a school) that had no rules...
> -or-
> While traveling around the world, I came upon a place that had no rules.
> The people needed help in getting along with each other...

2. Have students illustrate their stories and combine them into a class book.

3. Link this activity to other units you might be doing, e.g. the civil rights movement, slavery, or rules about protecting the environment.

As homework, ask students to write about rules that are in current news events, rules in history, or arbitrary or unfair rules, e.g. segregation, apartheid.

HOMEWORK

ANECDOTE

In one kindergarten class, during a discussion of rules in the larger community, a girl raised her hand and said that there could be unfair rules.

When asked to explain, she said that Rosa Parks helped to change a rule that was unfair and "mean," because black and white people couldn't be friends and couldn't even drink from the same water fountains.

LESSON TWO: CREATING RULES FOR THE CLASSROOM

Students create a set of rules for their classroom that will help them feel welcome, comfortable, and safe.

K-3 Activity: Brainstorming and writing rules (1 class session)

MATERIALS NEEDED: Chart paper; markers

1. Ask students, "What do you hope this year will be like?" "What do you want to learn?" List students' ideas on a class chart.

 TEACHER TIP:

When creating the chart, be sure to use all the ideas students come up with, writing them down in their own words. Older students can write their ideas on slips of paper, which can be taped to chart paper to use for discussion.

2. Review the chart with the class. Ask students, "What does the classroom need to be like to make these hopes and wishes come true?"

3. Use these suggestions as the framework for creating a set of rules for the classroom.

4. Help students create a rationale for the rules (the "whys"). It might take the form of a preamble to the rules, e.g., "To make our classroom a welcoming, comfortable, and safe place, we pledge to follow these rules."

5. Have students help sort the ideas on the chart into general categories of rules, for example:

> Kindness
> Cooperation
> Safety
> Respect for one another: girls for boys, boys for girls
> Students respecting adults
> Adults respecting students
> Respect for space and property
> Appropriate language
> Resolving conflicts without violence

6. Rewrite the list, using the categories as headings.

7. When the set of rules has been created, discuss how they will put the rules into action, and what the consequences of not following the rules will be.

8. Decide with students how to display the rules in the classroom. Students may have ideas for decorating the rules chart. Let students decide where their rules chart should be mounted.

9. As a final step, you can write up the list as a "contract," which you and the students sign. Copies of the "contract" can be sent home.

➤ **TEACHER TIP:**

To help students understand that there is more to a rule than writing it down, make a plan together to review the rules and the reasons we need them on a regular basis (daily or weekly). New rules may need to be added throughout the year. In particular, observe interactions between boys and girls and talk about rules that promote better understanding and respect. If you have observed any gender differences around rules, use them as a springboard for discussion with students.

Sample: Rules from a Kindergarten

Don't say bad words like stupid,
it hurts people's feelings
Don't get other kids in trouble

Sample: Rules from a Third Grade

Believe what people say
Answer your classmates' questions in a friendly way
Don't provoke, chase, spy!
If you are curious ask AND respect the answer
Trust your friends
Don't exclude, or give a kind reason
Let people play without following them
Explain in a respectful way

1-2 Activity: Creating a rules quilt (1 class session)

MATERIALS NEEDED: Paper or index cards; markers; masking tape or glue

1. This activity can be done individually or in pairs. Give out pieces of paper or index cards.

2. Have all the students illustrate one of their classroom rules. Students can write a sentence or two about their pictures, or they can create a picture without any words.

3. Gather the drawings and go over them with the class. Are any rules missing? If so, ask for a volunteer to illustrate that rule.

4. Using masking tape or glue, paste the pieces together into a Classroom Rules Quilt. The quilt can be used as part of a school-wide display.

ANECDOTE

In one class, the teacher specifically asked students to make their pictures without using any words. As a result, she felt that the students thought more about the messages that were conveyed by their pictures.

One Section of a Third Grade Rules Quilt

LESSON THREE: RULES OUTSIDE THE CLASSROOM

Students think about rules in the context of the school, community, and world.

K-1 Activity: Rules for a friendly playground (1 class session)

MATERIALS NEEDED: Large paper for poster; markers; half sheet of drawing paper for each student

1. Ask students to close their eyes and picture the school playground.

> What do they see?
> Is it a friendly place? Why? Why not?
> Do people fight? What about?
> Is the playground a place where people tease each other?

2. After the discussion, ask students if they can think of some rules that would make the playground a friendlier place.

3. Write the "Rules for a Friendly Playground" on a large sheet of paper using different colored markers.

4. Give out the half sheets of drawing paper and ask students to draw pictures of a friendly playground.

5. Attach the pictures around the edge of the "Rules for a Friendly Playground" poster.

6. Mount the poster in the classroom. If the playground becomes unfriendly, refer back to the poster.

1-2 Activity: All-school rules poster project (1-2 class sessions)

MATERIALS NEEDED: A copy of your school's rules; large paper for posters; markers

1. Once students have created their classroom rules, ask them:

> Should any of our classroom rules be for the whole school?
> Are there any others you would add?

2. If there are published school rules, share them with the students. Focus on the ones that address how people treat each other. Talk about the language of the rules. Ask students how the way the rules are written make them feel. If rules are not written in student-friendly language, students could work together to rephrase the rules in their own words and to incorporate the reasons. For example:

> "Hitting is not allowed" might become, "Hitting is not allowed because it hurts your feelings and your body,"
> - or -
> "We pledge not to hit or push or shove because it does not feel good."

3. Have the class brainstorm about what kinds of posters would give student-friendly messages about the school rules.

4. Have students work in pairs or in small groups to create posters that will illustrate the all-school rules. Display the posters on the school bulletin board or in the school entryway.

5. If it does not already exist, have students create an all-school rule about boys and girls showing respect for one another.

*In our school, girls and boys learn
to respect each other.*

1-2 Activity: Connecting home/school/community rules (1 class session)

MATERIALS NEEDED: None

1. To help students understand rules in a larger context, have the discussion develop in a progression from home, to school, to community. Ask:

> Why do we have rules at home? at school? in the community?
> Who makes the rules at home? at school? for the community?
> What happens if you break rules in your family? at school? in the community?

➤ **TEACHER TIP:**

This discussion can be very revealing. Students may bring up physical punishment. Be sure to plan ahead about how you might respond to a student who may talk about getting hit as punishment for breaking a rule at home.

2. Talk about how different rules apply in different situations. For example, loud voices are okay in a playground but not at home, in school or in a library; talking to people in your neighborhood is okay, but not to strangers in a different neighborhood; it's okay to accept food from family members or close friends, but never from people you don't know. Ask students:

> How do you know what the rules are?
> Are the rules different for girls and for boys? Is this fair? Why? Why not?
> Why do we have different rules for different situations/places?
> Why do we need to know these differences? What are the consequences if we don't?

For homework have students conduct research on rules in earlier times. They can ask older relatives about rules when they were in school or read a book about children who lived in earlier times.

2-3 Activity: Writing about an ideal world (1 class session)

MATERIALS NEEDED: Chart paper; writing paper; markers; pencils

1. Explain to students that they are going to be thinking about what it would take to make an ideal world and that this kind of place is sometimes called a "utopia" — "a place of ideal perfection, especially in laws, government, and social conditions."

2. On the top of a piece of chart paper write, "An Ideal World." Ask students:

> What do you think would need to happen if we wanted to have an ideal world?
> Would teasing and bullying exist in this world?
> How would boys and girls treat each other?
> Write their ideas on the chart paper.

3. Ask each student to contribute a sentence or two to a class story about a world where there is no teasing and bullying and where girls and boys are good friends.

4. As a class, create a set of rules that would need to exist in such a place.

As a homework assignment, ask students to relate the classroom work on rules to the larger world. How does the breakdown of rules affect countries getting along with each other? Have them find examples in the current news.

Problem Solving

K-3 Activity: Telling not tattling (10-15 minutes per segment)

MATERIALS NEEDED: Vignettes

Students need opportunities to discuss appropriate consequences for breaking the rules, and to problem-solve solutions as a class. Many students will be concerned about "snitching" or being a "tattletale." Distinguishing between telling and tattling is not always an easy thing to do.

Before the discussion, you may want to have the class agree on some guidelines. For example:

> Telling is reporting if someone is doing something harmful or on purpose.
> Telling is when you or someone else needs protection or when you are scared.
> Tattling is trying to get someone in trouble.
> Tattling is trying to get attention.

K-1 Vignettes

Read the vignettes aloud and ask students to decide whether they think the child in the story is "telling" or "tattling."

MEG AND PETER

Meg and Peter are building large towers in the block area. Peter's tower falls down. He knocks over Meg's tower and says, "Your tower fell down, too!" Meg asks Peter to stop it and starts to build her tower again. Peter knocks it down again and starts kicking the blocks around. One of the blocks hits Meg on the leg. Meg goes to tell her teacher what has happened.

> **Is this tattling or telling? Why?**
> **What else can Meg do?**
> **What would you do?**

THE COOKIES

The teacher puts the snack tray by the door to be picked up later. David sees Jesse take two cookies from the tray and goes to tell the teacher.

> **Is this tattling or telling? Why?**
> **What else can David do?**
> **What would you do?**

THE INSULT

Class 205 had made a set of class rules. One important rule was that boys and girls should respect each other. Every day at recess, two boys came up behind one girl and whispered an insult, which hurt her feelings. They whispered on purpose because they knew they were breaking the class rule. One day, another boy who was friends with the girl in school and in their neighborhood, saw her looking sad and asked what was wrong. The girl told him about what happened. The boy went back into the classroom before recess was over and told the teacher about the teasing.

Was he tattling or telling?
Do you agree with his solution?

1-2 Vignettes

Give out the Pam's Problem and Breaking a Rule vignettes. Students can work in pairs or individually to answer the questions.

PAM'S PROBLEM

Noemi collects small animal figures. She saves her allowance for weeks to buy them. Today she brought two new ones to school to show her friend, Pam. Before recess, Pam sees another student slip her hand into Noemi's backpack and take one of the animal figures. Pam stays back from recess to tell the teacher.

Is it telling or tattling?
How do you know?

BREAKING A RULE

There is a school rule that says no candy is allowed to be eaten, except on special occasions. One day Hannah comes to school with a favorite candy bar in her pocket. On the playground, she shows the candy to her friend, Robbie, and offers him a piece. Robbie says, "No thanks," and walks away. James is nearby and sees Hannah eat a piece of the candy bar.

Would James be tattling or telling if he reported that Hannah broke a rule?
How do you know?
What would you do?

2-3 Vignette

Give out the 4-Square Game vignette. Students can work in pairs to answer the questions.

THE 4-SQUARE GAME

One of the favorite recess activities at the Smithfield School is the ball game 4-square. Tamika loves to play, and she is good at it! Yesterday, she and her friends Kieko and Julie got to the 4-square court first and started to play with their friend Zack. Before long, lots of kids had gathered around to watch and cheer.

Julie was the first to get bounced out. Another boy, Nick, took her place. At first things went along as usual, then Nick hit a bomber to Kieko and she was out. Nick called Jonathan to take her place. The boys hit the ball back carefully to each other, but hit bombers to Tamika.

> **Was it fair that Nick, Jonathan, and Zack only hit "bombers" to the girls? Why/Why not?**
> **If Zack is Tamika's friend, why didn't he tell the other boys to stop? Why do you think he went along with them?**
> **What could an adult have done to help?**

Finally, Tamika was out, too. Nick raised his fist and shouted, "Boys rule!"

Tamika looked over at Zack. He kept his eyes down on the ground and seemed uncomfortable, but didn't say anything.

Now that Tamika was out, the boys hit the ball carefully so none of them were bounced out. They continued to play uninterrupted until the recess bell rang.

> **What rules would you make so this won't happen again?**
> **If you were one of the kids watching, what could you have done?**
> **Should Tamika have told the teacher or another adult what happened?**

Literature Connections

K-3 Activity: The Story of Ridley — A Place with No Rules
Baum, Frank. *The Wizard of Oz*. New York: Holt, Rinehart & Winston, 1982 ed.
Carroll, Lewis. *Alice's Adventures in Wonderland*. New York: St. Martin's Press, 1976 ed.
Seuss, Dr. *The Butter Battle*. New York: Random House, 1984.
Van Allsburg, Chris. *Jumanji*. Boston: Houghton Mifflin, 1981.

Connecting with Families

1. Send a letter home to let parents know that the class has been learning about rules — why we have them and why rules are important in school, at home, and in the community. (See sample Family Activity Letter.)

2. Invite parents and other family members in to see the rules that the class has created. A discussion of the classroom rules, between you, the student, and his or her parent, is a good way to connect with parents on these issues and will help to establish guidelines for everyone about appropriate classroom behavior for the school year.

3. At a parent-teacher meeting, talk with parents about classroom rules and behavior. Discuss how rules at school may now be very different from when parents, and you, were students. Acknowledge that rules may be different at home than at school, and explain the reasons for your classroom rules. Share with parents how students created their own rules and some of the class discussion around it.

4. Ask family members who are bilingual to help translate the rules into languages other than English.

Dear family member,

We have been creating rules for our classroom so that we will all feel welcome, comfortable, and safe. This would be a good opportunity for you to talk with your child about your rules at home. How are the rules different from rules that you had growing up? By discussing rules, you will encourage your children to stop and think about their behavior before they act.

Here are some ideas for further talks about rules:

✦ Play a "What if..." game. For example, how would you feel if:

> No one ever brushed their teeth?
> There were no rules about going to bed?
> There were no rules about taking care of toys, clothing, and other things that belong to you?
> People weren't nice to each other?
> People yelled and called each other names?

✦ Consider creating some new rules together about respecting and caring for others within the family and in the community. If you and your child create some new family rules, write them down in your child's own words. When the ideas and words are their own, children are more likely to follow the rules. Revisit the rules from time to time, adding new ones when necessary.

It's important to help your child understand that there are consequences if rules are not followed. Together, think of what some might be:

> If a safety rule is not followed, you might get hurt.
> If you are disrespectful, you may hurt someone's feelings and have your feelings hurt in return.
> If you break a rule, you may lose privileges like watching your favorite TV show or not going to a basketball game.

With regards,

_____

_____

_____

_____

_____

_____

_____

_____

_____

_____

_____

_____

_____

_____

_____

Talking About Teasing and Bullying

Kids can be friends if they don't tease each other.

– Kindergarten student

The children seemed more aware of certain behavior
such as pushing and derogatory comments.
They responded by saying, "That's not nice,"
but also used new vocabulary —
"That's like teasing," or "That's like bullying."

— First-grade teacher

In This Theme

LESSON ONE: I FEEL WELCOME/UNWELCOME

K-1 Activity: Story and drawing/writing
1-2 Activity: Pairs writing/chart and discussion
2-3 Activity: Personal writing and drawing
    Worksheets: I Feel Welcome ...,
               I Feel Unwelcome...,
               I Feel Welcome/Unwelcome...

LESSON TWO: WHERE I FEEL SAFE/UNSAFE

K-1 Activity: Brainstorming and mapping
1-3 Activity: Brainstorming, mapping, and discussion
2-3 Activity: Creating "Safety Zones"
    Worksheet: Creating Safety Zones

LESSON THREE: TEASING AND BULLYING ARE...

K-1 Activity: "I think"
1-2 Activity: Making anti-teasing and bullying posters
2-3 Activity: Thinking about teasing and bullying
2-3 Activity: Acts of kindness
    Worksheet: Think about Teasing and Bullying

LESSON FOUR: EXPRESSING OURSELVES

K-3 Activity: Talking/drawing/writing about being angry
1-2 Activity: Mood walks
1-2 Activity: Strong voices/looks
2-3 Activity: Be assertive

PROBLEM SOLVING

Puppets, role-plays, vignettes, stop-action stories
    Vignettes: The Jump Rope Game, Michael, Juan,
        Matt and Anna, Abby, Alex
    Worksheets: What Would You Do?, Take Action!

LITERATURE CONNECTIONS

CONNECTING WITH FAMILIES

    Take-home: Family Activity Letter

Goals

- To create a classroom climate that fosters open communication between students about teasing and bullying
- To have students define what constitutes teasing and bullying
- To have students assess the classroom and school climate in terms of teasing and bullying
- To empower students to convey a sense of strength and confidence through their voices, their bodies, and their expressions
- To help students cope with feelings of anger and frustration
- To help students recognize and assess the role gender and other factors play in teasing and bullying

Students Will Learn

- That teasing and bullying are not acceptable behaviors
- That the classroom is a safe space to talk about teasing and bullying
- That everyone has a broad range of feelings, but how we express them is important in how we get along with others
- That using their bodies to convey strength and confidence is one way to avoid being bullied
- How to recognize signs of their own anger
- Ways for boys and girls to treat each other that are fairer, friendlier, and more respectful

Background

Teasing and bullying are part of the "hidden curriculum" in many classrooms. By establishing clear ground rules that foster trust and respect among students early in the school year, you can minimize this behavior and its negative effect on your teaching and on student learning. When students have the opportunity to talk about teasing and bullying in a frank and candid manner, these important messages will be communicated:

Teasing and bullying are hurtful to everyone;

Teasing and bullying are not acceptable behaviors and will be met with clear consequences that are consistently implemented;

As teacher you are willing to intervene when problems arise, and any student can come to you for help;

The classroom is a safe place where students show respect for each other.

Creating a sense of belonging and commitment to the classroom and the larger school community helps students feel that the place where they spend a major part of their day is welcoming, comfortable, and safe. Factors such as age, gender, class, race/ethnicity, disability, and popularity — in addition to the amount of effective adult supervision available — all influence how students feel. However, when students are exposed to teasing and bullying they feel unsafe, uncomfortable, and excluded in the classroom as well as in other areas of the school.

In most schools, there are times of the day or specific areas where students feel particularly vulnerable, e.g., at lunch and recess, in the hallways and bathrooms, or on the playground. If you are able to observe during these high-risk times, you will gain a sense of the difficulties students face. You may be able to initiate some strategies to reduce stress around these potential trouble spots, e.g., engage students in developing solutions, provide more and better adult support, or develop school-wide policies.

In the activities that follow the words "unwelcome" and "unsafe" are used to introduce the way students may feel as a result of teasing or bullying by peers or older students. For younger students, in particular, the ideas of "accidentally" and "on purpose" should also be introduced into the discussion. For example, at first, something may be done accidentally, but if you ask someone to stop and they don't (or if someone asks you to stop and you don't), then it is on purpose. Students also need to understand that even if something is done accidentally, if it is hurtful to the other person, then it must stop.

Discussions are most effective when students are encouraged to talk about teasing and bullying in their own words. These words provide a framework for problem-solving solutions and taking action. For this reason, we recommend that teachers not define teasing and bullying for students but rather let them generate their own definition.

Activities in this theme will help integrate the topics of teasing and bullying into ongoing discussion. Also included are ideas to help students talk about what it feels like to be angry, and to express a variety of feelings through body language as well as words. It is important for students to be able to convey a sense of strength and confidence through their voices, their bodies, and their facial expressions.

LESSON ONE: I FEEL WELCOME/UNWELCOME

**Students explore what makes them feel welcome/unwelcome
and comfortable/uncomfortable in school.**

K-1 Activity: Story and drawing/writing (1-2 class sessions)

MATERIALS NEEDED: Copies of *I Feel Welcome When...* and *I Feel Unwelcome When...*
worksheets for each student; markers, crayons or pencils; red and green construction paper;
book: *Crysanthemum* (K, picture), *Rosie's Story* (K-3, picture/easy reader), *Oliver Button Is a Sissy*
(K- 2, picture); see Annotated Bibliography

PREPARATION: Select one of the books listed above and familiarize yourself with the story;
make copies of the worksheets.

1. Talk briefly about the words "welcome" and "unwelcome." Be sure students understand what the words mean.

2. Explain that you are going to read a book about what makes us feel welcome or unwelcome. Read the
story you have selected.

3. After the story, ask students:

Did the main character feel welcome or unwelcome?

What did the other characters do that made her/him feel that way?

What are some of the things that make you feel welcome? Unwelcome?

4. Give each student copies of the worksheets. Ask students to draw a picture of one thing that makes
her/him feel welcome one sheet, and one thing that makes her/him feel unwelcome on the other.
Encourage students to also write or dictate a sentence that describes their picture.

5. As an alternative, cut out circles of red and green construction paper (about 12 inches) to approximate
traffic lights. Have students draw welcome pictures on green and unwelcome on red. Mount the pictures as
stop/go lights and display them in the classroom.

〝〞 Sample: Kindergarten Responses

I feel welcome when...	I feel unwelcome when...
someone says play with me	someone says I don't care
someone is nice to me	someone pushes
I play with the teacher	someone says stupid
someone says Happy Birthday	someone's whispering

1-2 Activity: Pairs writing/chart and discussion (1-2 class sessions, plus a few minutes per day for adding to the list)

MATERIALS NEEDED: *I Feel Welcome/Unwelcome at School* **worksheet; chart paper and markers**

1. Introduce the activity by telling students that you are interested in knowing what makes them feel welcome in school. Be sure to tell them that each person's thoughts are important, and assure them that everyone will have a turn to speak.

2. Using the worksheets, ask students to work in pairs to write about what makes them feel welcome or unwelcome in school. They can write about the classroom, other places in the school, riding on the school bus, or walking to school.

 TEACHER TIP:

> **Set ground rules for the activity. For example, Do not interrupt when another student is speaking; Do not use actual names, describe someone as a girl or boy, older or younger student, adult, etc.; Do not write profane words, indicate them with a dash.**

3. Have students share their "welcome/unwelcome" situations with the group. Begin with the positive situations first. Write down what students say on a chart.

 TEACHER TIP:

> **It is important to write down what students say in their own words. Paraphrasing their words often can distort their meaning and even stifle discussion.**

4. Review the chart with students. Analyze the responses and group similar ideas together on the chart. Ask some questions to spur discussion:

> Did girls write about anything that made them feel especially welcome? Unwelcome?
> Did boys write about anything that made them feel especially welcome? Unwelcome?
> Were those things different for girls and boys?

ANECDOTE

During the pilot in a class discussion about differences in the ways that girls and boys annoy each other, students' responses included things like, "Boys hit, girls use their words," and "Boys chase, because that's what boys do."

5. If students don't introduce the words themselves, explain that some of what they have described is called "teasing" or "bullying." Have them think about how they feel when they are teased or bullied, so they understand that teasing and bullying are hurtful and are not allowed in the classroom or in the school.

6. Display the charts during the week for review, and spend a few minutes each day having students add something (be sure by the end of the week to have a comment from each student written down).

7. Brainstorm ways to make the classroom feel more welcoming. Refer to the classroom rules about getting along with each other. (See Theme 1: "Creating Our Rules.")

2-3 Activity: Personal writing and drawing (1 class session)

MATERIALS NEEDED: Paper and a variety of drawing materials

1. Ask students to work individually or in small student-selected groups.

2. Give students creative choices, such as writing and illustrating a story, drawing a comic strip, or designing a poster or mural that depicts something that makes them feel welcome or unwelcome in school.

3. Ask students to share their creations with each other. They also can create a bulletin board display.

TEACHER TIP:

Students' writing and pictures may be a reference point for further discussion. For example, if an incident arises that you know has been illustrated by one or more students, you can show the drawings as a way to open up a discussion. Gender issues may be reflected in the students' work, most likely through expressions of feelings of exclusion (in games, lunchroom seating arrangements, etc).

4. Talk about what makes girls and boys feel welcome or unwelcome. Be sure to highlight the stories and art work that illustrate positive as well as negative incidents.

I Feel Welcome

Name: _____   Date:_____

" I Feel Welcome When…"

_____

_____

_____

_____

_____

_____

I Feel Unwelcome

Name: _____ Date:_____

" I Feel Unwelcome When…"

_____

_____

_____

_____

_____

_____

I Feel Welcome/Unwelcome

Name: _____ Date:_____

" I feel welcome at school when…"

_____

_____

_____

_____

_____

" I feel unwelcome at school when…"

_____

_____

_____

_____

_____

LESSON TWO: WHERE I FEEL SAFE/UNSAFE

Students identify areas of the classroom and school where they feel safe and unsafe.

K-1 Activity: Brainstorming and mapping (2-3 class sessions)

MATERIALS NEEDED: Chart paper and markers (for brainstorming); blocks; small play figures, e.g., Lego or Playmobile (or "place-holders," such as colored cubes) — enough for each student to have two

BRAINSTORMING

1. Review students' responses to what makes them feel welcome and unwelcome in the school.

2. Tell students that you're interested in finding out about specific places in the classroom or in the playground where they feel welcome or safe, and places where they don't.

3. As students brainstorm, list the places on a sheet of chart paper.

CREATING A MAP OF THE CLASSROOM

4. Use blocks and the list of places students named during the brainstorming to build a structure to represent the classroom. Students also can build an area to represent the playground.

5. Give each student a small play figure or other "place-holder."

6. Ask students, one at a time, to put their figure inside the structure where they feel safe.

7. When all students have placed their "safe" figure, give each student another one to place where they feel unsafe.

8. Once students have placed their "safe" and "unsafe" figures, ask them to draw some conclusions from their "map":

> In what areas do kids feel most safe?
> Why do you think this is so?
> What areas feel most unsafe?
> What makes you feel unsafe in those places?
> What can we do to make those areas feel safer for everyone?

➤ **TEACHER TIP:**

Keep the structures up so that students can move their safe and unsafe figures around depending on what happens during the day. This can provide insight about how students are feeling and about classroom interactions from day to day.

9. Write students' ideas for ways to make the classroom and playground safer on chart paper. Ask them if their classroom rules could help.

10. Help students create a plan for how they can work together to make the classroom and playground safer places for everyone.

1-3 Activity: Brainstorming, mapping, and discussion (2-3 class sessions)

MATERIALS NEEDED: Chart paper and markers (for brainstorming); large sheet of brown paper for map (about 3' x 4' — the size of a bulletin board); green and red dot stickers (several of each per student) to use as safe and unsafe markers

BRAINSTORMING

1. Review students' responses to what makes them feel welcome and unwelcome in the school.

2. Tell students that you're interested in finding out about times during the day or specific places at school where they feel welcome or safe, and places where they don't.

3. Brainstorm all the places at school they use or walk through. List these places on a sheet of chart paper. Be sure to guide the discussion so that students include your classroom, other classrooms, lunchroom, auditorium, playground, gym, bathrooms, hallways, principal's office, nurse's room, lining-up areas, etc. Read through the list to make sure it includes all the places in the school that are familiar to students.

MAPPING

4. Using the large sheet of brown paper and the list of places students know about, have students create a map of the school that includes all the places on their list.

 TEACHER TIP:

If students are unfamiliar with using a map, explain that it is a kind of picture or diagram of a specific place — like your school. Since the purpose of this activity is to help students, and you, visualize where trouble spots might be, the map does not have to be to scale or completely accurate. You and students can approximate size and location of different rooms.

5. Students can work in small groups to draw the areas on the map.

6. Give each student one or two green and red dots. They can label each with their name or initials.

7. Ask students, one at a time, to place a green dot on the map in an area where they feel safe.

8. Then have students take the red dots and place them where they feel unsafe. Continue until all students have had a chance to participate.

• •

NOTE: *As an alternative to drawing a map you can put an outline of the classroom on the floor with masking tape and then have students use green and red blocks to "place" themselves where they feel safe (green) and unsafe (red). Students can then move the blocks around depending on what happens during the day.*

• •

DISCUSSION

9. Once your map is complete, follow with a discussion so students can draw some conclusions about why some places feel safe and others are "problem areas." Use the following questions as a guide to facilitate the discussion:

> What do you notice about our map?
> What does it tell us about where you feel safe and unsafe?
> Are there places where you feel most safe? Most unsafe?
> What makes you feel unsafe in these areas?
> What goes on there?
> Does anyone feel safe in these areas?
> Are they older? Boys? Girls?
> Do some places feel safe sometimes and not others? Why?
> Does it make a difference if you are a boy or a girl? Why?
> Does it make a difference if you are older or bigger? Why?
> Is there anything we can do about the unsafe places?

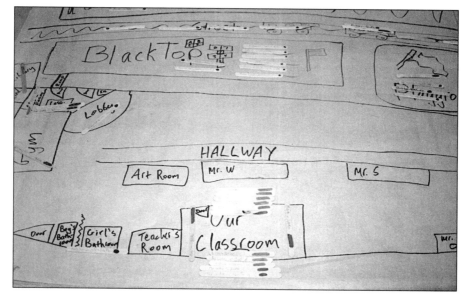

A First Grade Map with Safe/Unsafe Markers

2-3 Activity: Creating "Safety Zones" (1-2 class sessions)

MATERIALS/PREPARATION: If you have done the mapping activity, mount the map at student-eye level; make copies of the *Creating Safety Zones* worksheet for each student

1. This activity is effective as a small group cooperative project — divide students into groups of four. Explain to students that they are going to be problem-solvers — they are going to think about ways to help make the school a safer/more welcoming place for everyone. Some changes might happen immediately; others may take more time or planning to put into action.

2. Give each group a copy of the Creating Safety Zones worksheet, and review it to make sure that everyone understands the task. Refer students to the map they made, and assign each group an area of the school where students said they felt unsafe. (If you haven't done the mapping activity, spend some time brainstorming where students feel safe and unsafe at school.)

HOMEWORK **The Creating Safety Zones worksheet can be given as a homework assignment, followed by discussion in class.**

3. Ask each group to discuss reasons their assigned area feels unsafe and write their responses at the top portion of their worksheet. Ask them to consider:

> Who spends time in that place?
> Is it a particular group?
> Are they boys or girls?
> Are they older students?
> How does that influence other students' feelings about being safe or welcome?

4. Ask each group to brainstorm ways to make that place feel safer for all students. Ask them to include at least one idea of something that they can do to help. Have them write down their ideas on the worksheet.

5. Have each group report their ideas to the class.

6. Compile the student ideas into an action plan for the class.

7. Revisit the plan regularly to assess if students are feeling safer.

Creating Safety Zones

Name: _____ Date:_____

Problem Area: _____

_____

These are some of the reasons kids don't feel safe or welcome here:

1. _____

2. _____

3. _____

4. _____

Here are some ideas about how to make this problem area feel safer and more welcoming:

*(Remember to put a * next to things YOU can do to help).*

1. _____

2. _____

3. _____

4. _____

5. _____

LESSON THREE: TEASING AND BULLYING ARE...

Students address the meaning of teasing and bullying.

K-1 Activity: "I think" (1 class session)

MATERIALS NEEDED: Chart paper; markers

PREPARATION: On one large sheet of chart paper, write "I think teasing is..." as a heading. On another sheet, write the heading "Anti-teasing ideas..."

1. In a discussion group, tell students that you are interested in their ideas about teasing and bullying.

2. Ask students to take a moment and think about finishing this sentence: "I think teasing is..."

3. Give each student a turn and write down how he or she finishes the sentence. Be sure to write each student's name next to his or her sentence.

4. Discuss what students have said. Point out similarities and differences in their perceptions.

5. Read through the sentences together and ask students to think about how they might stop each of the teasing behaviors listed on the chart.

6. List student solutions on the "Anti-teasing ideas..." chart.

7. Mount both charts next to each other and revisit them periodically or as incidents of teasing occur.

1-2 Activity: Making anti-teasing and bullying posters (1 class session for discussion; 1-2 class sessions for poster-making)

MATERIALS NEEDED: Paper; markers; crayons for poster-making; "Be a Buddy Not a Bully" poster (optional; see Annotated Bibliography for ordering details)

1. Ask students to brainstorm: How can we get people to stop teasing and bullying?

2. Have students work individually or in small groups to plan and create their own anti-teasing and bullying posters.

3. Display the posters in the classroom or school hallway.

4. Expand on the activity by using the posters to start (or become part of) a school-wide anti-teasing and bullying campaign.

5. As an option, use the poster, "Be a Buddy Not a Bully," to provide inspiration for brainstorming and poster-making.

2-3 Activity: Thinking about teasing and bullying *
(brief introduction, plus 1-2 class sessions)

MATERIALS NEEDED: *Think about Teasing and Bullying* worksheet; chart paper; markers

PREPARATION: Make copies of the *Think about Teasing and Bullying* worksheet for each student.

INTRODUCTION

Tell students that you are interested in finding out what they know about teasing and bullying. Then distribute the worksheet, and go over it with students to see if they have questions.

HOMEWORK **Have students fill out the worksheet as homework.**

1. With their completed worksheets, divide the class into small groups and allow about 15 minutes for them to discuss their responses. Write questions on the chalkboard to help guide discussion:

> How did it feel to be teased or bullied?
> What were things you agreed were teasing or bullying?
> Did anyone disagree? Why?
> How did you know if something was teasing or bullying?
> What made you think so?

2. Ask each group to report back to the class. As the groups report, facilitate the discussion by asking:

> Do you all agree on what is teasing or bullying?
> Do boys and girls view the same behavior differently?

 TEACHER TIP:

Keep notes for yourself on student ideas and incidents to use as problem-solving scenarios.

3. Discuss the following questions with the group. Help students make the distinction that a bully isn't who you are, it's how you act. Sometimes the same person might act like a bully one minute and a friend the next. This will reinforce the idea that these are behaviors that we can change.

> What is a bully?
> Is a bully always a bully?
> Why do people tease?

4. Point out to students that they know a lot about teasing and bullying. Using their answers to the questions on the worksheet, work together to write definitions of teasing and bullying on chart paper to hang up in the classroom.

" Sample: 2nd Graders Talk about Why People Tease

To get attention
To make you mad
For revenge
Because they're bored
To get popular
Because they don't feel loved

" Sample: 3rd Grade Definition

Teasing is...	Bullying is...
saying bad things	pushing
pretending	making someone do something
saying false things	blackmailing, threatening

---

* This activity is adapted from one in L. Sjostrom and N. Stein, *Bullyproof: A Teacher's Guide on Teasing and Bullying for Use with Fourth and Fifth Grade Students* (Wellesley, MA: Center for Research on Women at Wellesley College and the NEA Professional Library, 1996).

2-3 Activity: Acts of kindness (5 10-minute sessions per day for journal writing; 1 class session for discussion/ charting/graphing)

MATERIALS NEEDED: Student journals; chart paper; markers

1. As students communicate with each other about teasing and bullying behavior — things they don't want to happen — remember that it is also important to have them think about positive behaviors — things they do want to happen. You can refer to these as "Acts of Kindness."

2. Tell students that for one week they are going to keep track of the ways students in the class treat each other. They will note acts of teasing and bullying and compare them to acts of kindness.

3. Ask students to keep a daily journal for five school days about what they observe. Ask them to note if they teased or bullied anyone, if they were teased or bullied, or if they saw anyone else being teased and bullied. Did they do anything when they saw someone else being teased and bullied? On a separate page, they should note their acts of kindness toward others, or when someone acted kindly toward them.

4. At the end of the week, ask if anyone would be willing to share specific examples of what they recorded. Tell students they should not use names when sharing negative examples.

5. Discuss what students observed and chart the kinds of incidents reported. Ask students:

> Based on what you observed, how do you feel about how we treat each other in school?
> Was there more teasing and bullying behavior or acts of kindness?
> Did anyone step in to stop teasing or bullying?
> Do girls and boys treat each other with respect?
> What can we do to help each other be more kind?

6. Make a graph of teasing/bullying incidents and acts of kindness reported by students. As a follow-up activity, repeat the week-long observations and graph them as well. Compare the two graphs to see if there have been changes in balance between teasing/bullying and kind acts.

• •

NOTE: *An alternative method is to give each student several index cards of different colors, which they can tape to their desk like a little book. They should record acts of teasing and bullying on one color card; and acts of kindness on the other. (The top card should be kept blank to keep notes private.)*

• •

Think about Teasing and Bullying

Name: _____ Date:_____

Think and write down your thoughts.

What is teasing?

_____

What is bullying?

_____

Have you ever been teased?

Describe one experience.

_____

_____

_____

How did you feel? Why?

_____

_____

_____

LESSON FOUR: EXPRESSING OURSELVES*

Students explore how they feel and act when they are angry and use their bodies to express a variety of feelings, both positive and negative.

K-3 Activity: Talking/drawing/writing about being angry
(2 class sessions)

MATERIALS NEEDED: Drawing and/or writing materials; book or video: *The Grouchy Ladybug* (K, picture book), *Matthew and Tilly* (K-1, picture book), *How to Lose All Your Friends* (K-3, picture book), *I Hate My Best Friend* (2-3, early reader), "All About Anger" (video), "A Rainbow of Feelings" (video), see Annotated Bibliography for additional selections

1. Start the discussion about anger by reading a book or showing a video from the list above.

2. During a group discussion, ask students:

Nia is feeling sad because everybody is teasing her in the playground.

> Do you ever get angry?
> What makes you angry?
> How do you feel inside when you get angry?
> How does your body feel when you are angry?
> What do you do when you get angry?
> Is it the same as when you are sad?
> What can you do to calm down when you get angry?

3. Have students draw and/or write about a time they were angry, including what caused their anger, what happened as a result, and how they calmed down. Older students can write skits and act them out. Schedule extra time on subsequent days for students to act out their skits.

>
>
> **TEACHER TIP:**
>
> **This activity provides an opportunity for students to talk about a subject that is often avoided. You can use the activity to gain insight into the sources of students' anger and help them develop strategies for coping. It is important to accept all student responses without censoring them. Use student responses as a springboard to discuss possible alternatives and to help students explore the pros and cons of various responses. Outlets for angry feelings can be expressed through puppets, role-plays, dramatizations, drawing, dictating, or writing.**

---

* The activities in this lesson are based on the work of the Children's Empowerment Project of the Center for Anti-Violence Education in Brooklyn, New York.

1-2 Activity: Mood walks (1 class session)

PREPARATION: No materials are needed. A large open area, such as a gym or outdoor space, is best for this activity. If possible, do this activity with half the class at one time.

1. Ask students to sit in a circle on the floor.

2. Explain that they will be acting out different moods with their bodies, without using any words. Introduce vocabulary words "mime" and "pantomime."

3. Choose a mood, e.g., happy or angry, as an example, and model how you would look if you were expressing that mood. Ask students:

> How am I standing?
> What am I doing with my arms? Head? Shoulders?
> How do my eyes look? My eyebrows?
> Does my body look tense or relaxed?
> Can you guess my mood by the way I look?

4. Ask students to rearrange themselves so they are sitting side by side in two rows facing each other.

5. Ask for student volunteers to walk down the path showing that they are as happy as can be. Then ask some students to walk in a way that would let others know that they are angry.

6. Have students take turns acting out different moods/emotions/feelings. You may want to suggest a scenario to act out:

> You're playing a fun game with a friend.
> - or-
> You see a kid who has been grabbing your hat in the schoolyard and you feel really angry or anxious.

Acknowledge that the same scenario can elicit different emotions for different people.

7. Continue to let students take turns demonstrating other feelings with their bodies as they walk between the two rows.

8. After each demonstration, talk about the body language the student has used.

> How did you know Tim was scared?
> What did his eyes look like?
> Were his shoulders straight or slumped?
> How did you know Ellie was feeling confident?
> How did her shoulders look?
> Did she walk fast?
> Did she look straight ahead?

9. Have students form two lines at opposite ends of the room facing each other. Have one line watch as the other group walks toward them and between them in the strongest and most confident manner. Then switch lines.

10. After everyone has a turn, return to sitting in a circle. Ask students:

> What makes someone look strong and confident?
> How do they hold their head? Their hands? Their shoulders?
> How did it make you feel to walk in a strong and confident manner?
> Is it the way you usually walk?
> Can you feel scared but act confident? How?

11. Relate the activity to teasing and bullying. Ask:

> Do bullies pick on people who look strong and confident?
> Do bullies pick on people who look timid and scared?
> How can changing your body language help you avoid being teased or bullied?
> Can you be scared and walk like you're really strong?

1-2 Activity: Strong voices/looks (1 class session)

PREPARATION: No materials are needed. You will need to find a space where students can use loud voices, e.g., outdoor space or gym. If possible, do this activity with half the class at one time.

1. Ask students to scrunch up very close together in a small space for a few seconds.
Then have them move an arm's length apart. Ask:

> Did it feel better when we were all scrunched together or when we moved farther apart?

2. Explain that sometimes people need to "set limits" so they can stop unwanted behavior and feel more comfortable or safer. Talk about how our eyes or voices can be used to be welcoming to someone else or to "set limits" and keep another person away.

3. Ask students to line up side by side and place yourself in front of them. Have students demonstrate using a welcoming look and voice. Ask:

> How would your voice sound if you wanted me to come and play with you?
> What kind of words would you use?
> How would you sound if you wanted to be friendly?
> How would you look?

As individual students demonstrate welcoming and friendly looks and voices, move close to them.

4. Next, stand close to students and ask them to try using strong looks, voices, and words to "push" you away. Tell them that they can only use their faces and voices, not their hands or bodies to make you move. Ask:

> How would your voice sound if you wanted to use it to push me away from you?
> What words would you use?
> How would you look?
> Would your eyes look friendly or angry?

As individual students demonstrate how they would use strong looks, voices, and words, move away from them.

5. Have students try the activity with a partner, first using welcoming, friendly looks, voices, and words; and then using strong looks, voices, and words to push their partner away. Let each partner try both aspects.

6. Discuss what happened. Ask:

> How did it feel when your partner used a welcoming look and voice?
> How did you feel when your partner used a strong look, voice, and words to push you away?
> How did it make you feel to use a strong look, voice, and words?
> What are some situations when you would want to use a strong look, voice, and words?

7. Tell students that using a strong voice or look is one way to be assertive, to stand up for yourself without hitting or hurting anyone.

2-3 Activity: Be assertive (1 class session, plus reading and journal writing)

MATERIALS NEEDED: Book: *The Hundred Dresses* (3, early reader, chapter book), *Babe the Gallant Pig* (3+, chapter book), or other selection from Annotated Bibliography about problem-solving and/or teasing and bullying; or film, *"Molly's Pilgrim* (2-4);" student journals

1. Review the terms "body language," "aggressive," and "assertive" to be sure students understand their meaning.

2. Have the class read one of the stories or watch a film listed above.

3. Hold a class discussion about the film or story. Ask:

> How did the main character react to the bully?
> Was the main character assertive? Aggressive? Neither?
> Can you describe ways in which any of the characters in the story (or film) were assertive?
> In what ways did the bully show her or his power?

4. Assign a journal writing activity. Ask students to:

> Choose a character from the story — a bully, target, or bystander
> Think about how that character could have used assertive behavior to change the story
> Write a new ending

5. Ask for volunteers to share their new endings.

6. Have a class discussion about real-life situations where being assertive could be helpful. Be sure to also include discussion of situations where it would be unwise, and talk about alternatives, e.g., seeking adult help, running away.

As a creative writing assignment, ask students to write about: 1) A teasing or bullying situation; 2) an assertive response to the situation; and 3) the outcome or consequences. Have them discuss whether the assertive response was a wise or unwise choice.

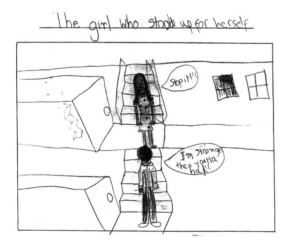

Problem Solving

Puppets/role-plays/stop-action stories/vignettes (see Problem-Solving Techniques section for descriptions of how to use)

MATERIALS NEEDED: *What Would You Do?* **worksheet for use with puppets or role-play (K-2);** *Take Action!* **worksheet for use with stop-action stories (2-3); vignettes**

Students need practice to help them learn ways of responding to teasing and bullying situations that are realistic and that will keep them safe. Regardless of which approach to problem-solving you use, encourage students to consider these possible actions:

> They can learn to walk away (to avoid confrontation).
> They can learn ways to divert a bully's attention (to diffuse the situation).
> They can learn to negotiate or find a compromise (to resolve a conflict).
> They can learn how and when to stand up for themselves (to assert themselves).
> They can learn how and when to seek adult help (to protect themselves).

You may want to begin by asking students which of these options they think would work best. Rather than critiquing or judging the solution, help students think it through to its logical conclusion and discuss its pros and cons. For example, if a student proposes hitting back as a solution, ask what might happen as a result of this action:

> Would it stop the bully?
> Could you get hurt?
> Would the conflict escalate?
> Would you get in trouble for hitting?

Then, as a group, talk about whether hitting is a good idea. Would there be a better chance to work things out if a different solution was tried instead? You can have younger students note their solutions on the What Would You Do? worksheet, which presents three options that students can check off. For older students, the Take Action! worksheet is a tool to help them make choices and explain their reasoning.

The mean boy was saying bad words to me.
I was feeling very sad
I ran away because I didn't like him.

K-1 Puppet or Role-Play

David, Linda, and Louis are working at one table. David grabs Linda's pencil. Linda says, "Give it back. I need it." David says, "No way," and he laughs. Louis says, "Give it back, it's hers." Linda looks very upset, but does nothing. Louis tries to grab the pencil from David.

K-1 Puppet or Role-Play

Danielle always wants to play with Bobby. She sticks close by, she interrupts his games with others and taps him on the shoulder to get his attention. Bobby thinks Danielle is a pest. He tries to find ways to keep away from her, but she won't leave him alone.

1-2 Puppet or Role-Play

At recess, dodge ball is a very popular game. But, Kim is never invited to play. She just stands on the side watching. One day, a really good player, Julie, decides to let Kim into the game, and the other kids protest. They yell, "She doesn't even know how to play."

2-3 Stop-Action Stories

✦ During recess, boys steal girls' jump ropes and toss them over the fence.

✦ Someone you don't like asks you to play and won't take no for an answer.

✦ You want a turn on the tire swing, but two students (who have been swinging for a long time) say you can't.

K-1 Vignette

THE JUMP ROPE GAME

At recess, Ellen and Mitsu set up a jump rope game. Amy and two other girls come over and join in. Amber comes over and says, "Can I play?" Ellen and Mitsu yell, "You can't play, you're too fat to jump rope." Amber tries to push into the jump rope line. Ellen and Mitsu try to stop Amber. Ellen says, "Get off the line. It's our game and we said you can't play." Amy says, "Let her play."

       Were Ellen and Mitsu being fair?
       How do you think Amber felt?
       Was Amy a bystander? What did she do?
       Was there anything else Amy could have done?

K-1 Vignette

MICHAEL

Michael, a kindergartner, climbs onto the school bus. Three older boys are already on the bus. The older boys tease Michael all the way to school. They call, "baby," and yell out to other kids who are getting on the bus, "watch out for baby, baby wears diapers." Some of the students on the bus look around at each other. Finally, one boy says, "Cut it out, he's a little kid." But the teasers keep right on. Michael has tears in his eyes as he gets off the bus and runs into school.

Were the older boys being fair to Michael?
Why were they teasing him?
Were the other students on the bus bystanders? What could they have done?
Did anyone try to help Michael?
What else could the students do to stop the teasing?

1-2 Vignette

JUAN

It's a beautiful day and all the children are outside for recess. When Juan sees a group of children from his class playing a running game, he runs to join them. When he gets there, the group scatters and moves away. Lionel tells Juan, "You can't play with us. We don't play with brown kids!" Juan can't believe his ears — Lionel lives across the street from Juan and plays with him every day after school! Juan thought they were good friends.

Why do you think the children acted this way?
Why does Lionel play with Juan at home but act like this at school?
What would you do if you saw this happen?
How do you think Juan feels?
If you were part of the group of children, what could you do?

2-3 Vignette

MATT AND ANNA

Part One

Matt, a third grader, walks to school with his little sister, Anna, a kindergartener. A group of fifth-grade girls hang out on the corner near school.

> Are there places around school or the neighborhood where certain groups of kids hang out?
> How does it feel when you have to go there?

The girls often stop Matt and Anna and talk to them. The older girls giggle when Anna talks and tell her how cute she is. Sometimes, Matt thinks they are making fun of Anna, but she smiles and giggles and doesn't seem to mind. So he doesn't say anything.

> Why do kids laugh when they are being teased?
> Should Matt ignore the girls' teasing?

Part Two

Lately, the girls have been surrounding Matt and Anna so they can't walk away when they talk to them. Once or twice, Matt and Anna have even been late for school because the girls blocked their way. Yesterday, one of the girls asked Anna what she'd brought for lunch. Before Matt knew what happened, the girl took Anna's cupcake. Matt tried to get it back, but the older girls just laughed and held it over his head. When the girls walked away, Anna started crying. Matt hugged her until she calmed down and gave her the cupcake from his own lunch. Matt felt mad at the girls, but wasn't sure what else he could have done.

> Why do you think the girls are acting this way?
> What can Matt do now? What are the advantages and disadvantages of each choice?
> Should Matt tell his parents what's going on? What could they do to help?

Part Three

Today, the girls stopped Matt and Anna again. Matt held Anna's hand hard and tried to push his way through the girls, but they wouldn't let him.

Matt yelled at them to move, but they just laughed. Then, one of the girls took Matt's lunch box and started tossing it around. Another girl pushed Matt. Anna kicked her. Matt was scared, but he grabbed Anna and pushed the older girl away. "Leave us alone," he yelled. "I don't want to fight." "What's the matter, scaredy cat?" the girls jeered. "Are you afraid to hit a girl? The wuss lets his baby sister fight for him." The girls left, spilling Matt's lunch all over the sidewalk. Matt felt mad at himself, mad at Anna, and mad at the girls.

> Why did the girls call Matt a baby and a wuss?
> Why didn't the girls move when Matt told them to?
> Should Matt have hit the girl or started a fight?
> Should Anna be punished for kicking the girl?
> Is it ever OK to get into a fight?
> What do you think will make the older girls stop tormenting Matt and Anna?

ABBY

Part One

Abby and her friends can't wait for recess. Every day, Abby and a large group of girls bring jump ropes from home. They gather on the blacktop and practice double dutch routines. Usually, the boys play ball games with balls they bring from home.

One day, part way through recess, a few of the boys ran up and stepped on the ropes just as the girls were jumping. This continued for about 10 minutes. The girls shouted at the boys to stop, but the boys just laughed and ran away. Soon, the bell rang and it was time to return to class. The next day, the boys started grabbing and stepping on the girls' ropes just as they began jumping. Abby and her friend Daniella complained to one of the playground aides. The aide told them to work it out with each other. When the girls returned to their game, one of the boys made faces and yelled, "Crybaby!" and "Sissies!" at Abby and Daniella. The girls tried to ignore them.

> Is calling someone a sissy a compliment or a put down?
> How do the girls feel?
> Do you agree with what the aide told them? Why/why not?
> Do you think the girls should have done something different to stop the boys?

Part Two

Over the next week, things got worse. As soon as the girls got out their ropes, the boys grabbed them. At first, the boys played tug-of-war or pretended to tie each other up with the ropes. But when the girls chased the boys or tried to get their ropes back, the boys threw them over the fence into the woods. The girls knew they couldn't get their ropes back because the woods were off-limits to the students. Once again, the girls complained to the aide. She told them, "I'm tired of your whining and tattling all the time. You need to work this out yourselves."

The next day, the boys continued to take the ropes. By the end of the day, all but two of the ropes had been tossed over the fence. In tears, several of the girls complained to their teacher about what had happened. She said, "If you can't find a way to get along with the boys, leave your jump ropes at home! Find another game to play so they won't tease you."

> How do the girls feel now?
> What would you do if you were one of the boys?

Part Three

On Monday morning, Mr. Brock, the principal made an announcement. He said, "I've heard many complaints about the problems that jump ropes are causing on the playground. I have been told that some students are using the ropes to tie each other up and that ropes are being thrown over the fence into the construction site. From now on, jump ropes will not be permitted on school property." The boys in the class made faces, laughed, and gave each other the thumbs-up sign.

> Do you think the principal's solution was fair? Why/why not?
> If you were the principal at Abby's school, what would you do?

2-3 Vignette

ALEX

Part One

Alex just started third grade. He and his parents and little sister just moved to Newville. His parents are thrilled about their new house and neighborhood, but Alex is miserable.

The kids at Alex's new school mostly just ignore him. This week, Josh, one of the popular fifth graders, started making jokes about Alex's ears. In the hallway, before school, Josh yelled, "Look out, here comes Dumbo! He's flying low!" It seemed that everyone stopped and stared at Alex.

Brian, a fourth grader, told Josh, "Lay off him! He's not doing anything!" But Josh just laughed and told Brian to mind his own business. Several other boys started laughing and threw themselves face down on the floor yelling, "Look out for Dumbo," and "Hit the deck!"

Alex felt his face get hot as tears started to fill his eyes. Somehow he made it to his locker and put his stuff away.

> Has anything like this ever happened to you?
> Have you ever seen anything like this happen to someone else?
> How did it make you feel?
> Why do you think Josh didn't listen to Brian?
> Do you think Brian could have done anything else to help Alex?

Part Two

Every night, Alex's mom asks him about school. He usually just says, "Fine." His mom tells him how lucky they are to be living in such a nice neighborhood with such a great school. She suggests that Alex invite some friends over to play after school.

> Why do you think Alex doesn't tell his mom what's really going on?
> If you were Alex, what would you do?

Part Three

At lunch, the third graders all sit in one area of the cafeteria. Usually the girls sit together at a table near the door, and the boys sit together near the windows. Alex dreads lunch.

Whenever Alex tries to sit in an empty place at one of the boy's tables, the boys tell him, "Sorry, this seat is saved." When he finally manages to find a seat, the boys move away. He sees them pulling on their ears and laugh at him. The girls whisper and laugh, too. A few of the kids look uncomfortable, but they don't say anything.

> **Why do you think Alex doesn't say anything to the boys?**
> **What do you think would happen if he told a teacher what was happening?**
> **If some of the kids feel uncomfortable about what's happening to Alex, why don't they say anything?**

Part Four

Now, things are getting worse. Today, as he was finishing his lunch, several of the boys secretly flicked his ears as they walked past. He felt the tears filling his eyes again. He kept his head down and tried to concentrate on chewing.

> **If you were one of the kids who were watching, what could you have done?**

Alex didn't want to tell his teacher about what happened at lunch. Mr. Platt never seemed to see any of this anyway. Besides, Alex didn't want to be called a tattletale on top of everything else. The next day, Alex tells his mom he's sick and can't go to school.

> **Should he tell his parents what's going on?**
> **If you were Alex, what would you want your parents to do?**

What Would You Do?

Name: _____ Date:_____

My solution to the problem is:

Walk away	Stand up to the person	Get an adult

Take Action!

Name: _____ Date:_____

My solution to the problem is:

    1. I would walk away.

    2. I would stand up to the person who is teasing or bullying me (or someone else).

    3. I would go for help from an adult (or another student),

    4. I would try something else (negotiate, distract, etc.).

Story 1 Solution #_____

Reason:_____

_____

_____

_____

Story 2 Solution #_____

Reason:_____

_____

_____

_____

Story 3 Solution #_____

Reason:_____

_____

_____

_____

Literature Connections

K-1 Activity: Story and Drawing/Writing

Henkes, Kevin. *Crysanthemum*. New York: Greenwillow Books, 1991.
Gogoll, Martine. *Rosie's Story*. Greenvale, NY: Mondo Publishing, 1994.
dePaola, Tomie. *Oliver Button is a Sissy*. San Diego: Voyager/Harcourt Brace Jovanovich, 1979.

Additional Suggestions for Theme

Carlson, Nancy. *How to Lose All Your Friends*. New York: Puffin/Penguin Books, 1994.
    (K-3, picture).
Cosby, Bill. *The Meanest Thing to Say*. New York: Scholastic, 1997. (K-3, picture/easy reader).
Estes, Elinor. *The Hundred Dresses*. San Diego: Voyager/Harcourt Brace Jovanovich, 1972.
    (3, easy reader/chapter).
Little, Jean. *Jess Was the Brave One*. Toronto: Viking, 1991. (K-1, picture).
Petty, Kate and Charlotte Firmin. *Being Bullied*. Hauppauge, NY: Barron's, 1991.
    (K-1, picture).

Connecting with Families

1. Share the map-making experience with families. Suggest that this might be a good way to help them talk to their children about where they feel safe and unsafe in their neighborhoods.

2. If students have made drawings or written stories, send them home with a note explaining about the activity and suggesting that family members ask their children to talk about what they have drawn or written.

3. If you use any of the worksheets as homework, suggest that family members help their children fill it out.

Dear family member,

We have been talking about teasing and bullying in our classroom. We want your child to feel comfortable talking about this topic openly in the classroom. We hope you will encourage your child to talk about teasing and bullying behavior at home, too.

Here are some ways you can help:

+ Remember hitting back is not a choice at school.

+ Teach your child to walk in a confident manner.

+ Encourage your child to walk away and tell an adult if he or she feels someone is about to hurt her or him.

+ With your child, practice using a strong voice or strong look. These are things we have practiced at school.

+ Talk about safe ways to act in situations that might be dangerous. For example, identify a safe house or store or walk with an adult or older child.

With regards,

Theme 3

Exploring Courage

*She's my friend. Stop teasing her.
It's mean to tease.*

– Second-grade student

While the children have been exposed to "courage" in many pieces of
literature that we've read, this allowed them to take the term and
relate it more to real-life situations. It certainly opened their eyes
to the many ways courage can be displayed.

— First-grade teacher

In This Theme

LESSON ONE: COURAGE IS...?

K-3 Activity: Story and discussion

1-2 Activity: Creating a courage pictures display

1-2 Activity: Finding a solution

2-3 Activity: It would take courage to...

LESSON TWO: DO THE RIGHT THING/LISTEN TO YOUR STRONG SIDE

K-1 Activity: We listen to our strong side

1-2 Activity: Poster campaign

2-3 Activity: Journal writing

2-3 Activity: Standing up for someone stories

LESSON THREE: BREAKING DOWN BARRIERS TO FRIENDSHIP

K-2 Activity: Building and problem-solving

2-3 Activity: Creative writing and performing

2-3 Activity: Writing friendship poems

Worksheet: The Friendship Poem

PROBLEM SOLVING

Puppets, role-plays, stop-action stories

LITERATURE CONNECTIONS

CONNECTING WITH FAMILIES

Take-home: Family Activity Letter

Goals

- To explore the meaning of courage, including acts that can happen on a daily basis
- To examine the role courage plays in helping to stop teasing and bullying behavior
- To develop courageous strategies to stop teasing and bullying behavior
- To explore the role and responsibility that bystanders have in incidents of teasing and bullying
- To help students recognize barriers to friendship, including stereotypes about gender, race/ethnicity, disability, and other perceived differences

Students Will Learn

- That everyone has a responsibility to stop teasing and bullying
- That using violence to solve problems is not courageous
- How to differentiate between being courageous and taking unsafe risks
- That they can think of solutions to conflicts and practice ways of responding to teasing and bullying that are not aggressive or hurtful to others
- That they can recognize some barriers to friendship and develop ways to eliminate them
- That breaking down barriers to friendship takes courage

Background

For many students, the concept of courage is closely tied to athletes or "super hero" programs, or even to commercials that depict acts of dangerous derring-do. Thanks to the wonders of computer-generated special effects and stunt performers, students see "heroes" jumping through windows, walking through fires, conducting high speed chases, jumping across roof tops, and always escaping unharmed. They learn that solving problems involves violence or taking unrealistic risks.

For the youngest students, who still are not always able to distinguish between fantasy and reality, this notion of "courage" can be particularly harmful. Preschool and kindergarten teachers often relate anecdotes about catching a student imitating super-hero behavior — even very risky maneuvers! As you might expect, since the majority of movie and television super-heroes are male, they may lead boys into taking unrealistic risks. During the pilot-testing of this Guide, one boy responded that he would "jump down from the plane and wipe out the bullies, just like Superman."

Students need to understand that there are many forms of courage, and heroes do not have to fight or rescue someone.

It takes courage not to "follow the crowd," especially at this young age when belonging is so important. If we can help students find their own inner strength in the early grades they will be better prepared to resist the peer pressure that becomes so intense in adolescence.

It takes courage to disagree with someone and risk that they might not be your friend.

It takes courage to go against the social norm and break down barriers to friendships between girls and boys. It is especially important to address these barriers in the early grades. Patterns of behavior established in the elementary grades can have many ramifications for adolescent and adult relationships between the sexes.

It takes courage to perform acts of kindness, especially when they involve overcoming a barrier or standing up for someone who is often a target of teasing or bullying. There are many factors that influence how easy or difficult it is to be courageous: your age; size; how popular you are; and whether you are a boy or a girl.

It takes courage to control your own emotions and not lash out. Helping students learn strategies to manage their anger can defuse teasing and bullying behavior and, at the same time, improve the student's self-esteem.

This theme helps students expand their more traditional views about courage. It promotes understanding about the many subtler meanings of courage in relation to daily classroom situations, especially around teasing and bullying behavior and standing up for someone who is in trouble without taking undue risks. There is a strong focus on how much courage it takes to "do the right thing" as a bystander and on breaking down stereotypes that are barriers to friendships. Concepts of courage are reinforced through writing, drawing, literature, discussions, and role-plays.

LESSON ONE: COURAGE IS…?

Students broaden their understanding of the term courage and identify daily actions that are courageous.

K-3 Activity: *Story and discussion (1 class session)*

MATERIALS NEEDED: Chart paper; markers; book: *Arnie and the Skateboard Gang* **(K-2, picture);** *Amazing Grace* **(1-2, picture/easy reader);** *Felita* **(3, chapter)**

1. Choose a book from the list above, each of which addresses everyday acts of courage (or select one from the Annotated Bibliography). Read the book (or passage from a book) aloud to students.

2. To facilitate the discussion, ask:

How did the characters in the stories deal with their fears?
What did they do to overcome their fears?
When you feel afraid what do you do to overcome your fears?
Can anyone tell me what the word "courage" means?
Did the characters in the story show courage? How?
Has anyone ever been in a situation where it took courage to respond?
Do you feel afraid when you see someone being bullied?
Do you think it would take courage to do something? What might you do?

3. If students' perceptions of courage are related to "super heroes" or to fighting, ask them to think back to the story and the way that the main character showed courage without using aggression or taking unwise risks.

4. Tie the discussion of courage to other areas the class might be studying, e.g., the civil rights movement and integration, peace movement, protecting the environment.

HOMEWORK Ask students to talk to an adult family member or friend about a time when she or he helped someone or stood up for someone *without using violence*. Students can tape record the answers, write them down, or retell them at a class meeting.

1-2 Activity: Creating a courage pictures display (2 class sessions)

MATERIALS NEEDED: Drawing paper; markers; bulletin board; stapler

1. Tell students that you would like to create a bulletin board display about courage to share with other classes in the school.

2. Ask students to draw a picture or a scene about standing up for someone who is being teased or bullied. Tell students that they can draw any scene they want, but stress that the picture can't show weapons or any form of violence. They can also write (or dictate) a sentence or two that describes the scene.

3. Design the bulletin board as a class. Students may want to include their definition of courage in the center of the display or use it as a heading. Let students make their own decisions about the display.

1-2 Activity: Finding a solution (1 class session)

MATERIALS NEEDED: "The Baseball Cap" (See below)

1. Read "The Baseball Cap" to the class. Personalize the story by adding details such as your hometown baseball team's name.

THE BASEBALL CAP

Cindy went to a major league baseball game with her family as a birthday celebration. Her presents, besides tickets to the game, were a team banner to hang over her bed and a baseball cap with the team logo. Cindy was very attached to her cap. She was a big fan of the hometown team (supply name). She listened to every game on the local radio station and ran for the newspaper every morning to get the scores.

Every day at recess Joe and Debby grabbed Cindy's baseball cap and ran away with it. This made Cindy very upset, and they knew it. Joe and Debby would laugh and tease Cindy as she tried to get the cap back. Sometimes, Cindy would have tears in her eyes, but she would not give up wearing her cap out to recess.

David, Amy, and Mike usually watched the chasing and teasing, and sometimes they laughed, too. But their class had been talking about teasing and bullying, and also about how much better it would be if people treated each other more kindly. The class had even made an "Acts of Kindness" chart for the bulletin board that hung outside their classroom.

One day, David, Amy, and Mike decided that they wanted the teasing to stop!

2. Have students come up with suggestions to stop the teasing. Vote on the idea most students think would work best.

3. Finish the story with the students' solution. The next day David, Amy, and Mike...

4. As a further discussion, ask students:

>How do you think Cindy felt at the beginning of the story? At the end?
>What might have happened if David, Amy, and Mike hadn't stepped in?
>Were they courageous? What did they do that was courageous?
>What if Joe and Debby had been older or bigger? What should David, Amy and Mike have done then?
>Could they have shown courage with a different solution?

2-3 Activity: It would take courage to... (1 class session)

MATERIALS NEEDED: Index cards; basket; student journals

PREPARATION: Write "It would take courage to..." in the center of a large piece of chart paper and hang it near the class meeting area.

1. Ask students to think about an example of teasing and bullying they know about. Tell them to keep their example in their mind, but don't say it aloud.

2. Give out the index cards, and ask each student to write down the incident they have thought about on one side of the card, using no names, e.g., I saw a girl get teased on the school bus..., or I saw two middle school boys chase some little kids down the block....

3. Ask students to place their cards in the basket. Shuffle the cards and ask each student to select one card.

4. On the back of each card, ask students to write, "It would take courage to..." and finish the sentence with one or more courageous solutions to the problem on their cards.

5. Ask students to read their problems and solutions aloud. If some of the solutions focus on risky or aggressive behavior, you might want to ask the student to rethink the situation and come up with some different ideas. Remind students of previous discussions about everyday types of courageous behavior that don't rely on high risk or aggression.

LESSON TWO:
DO THE RIGHT THING/LISTEN TO YOUR STRONG SIDE

Students generate different strategies to help someone in trouble.

K-1 Activity: We listen to our strong side (1 class session)

MATERIALS NEEDED: *JoJo's Flying Side Kick* (1-2, picture); chart paper; markers

**PREPARATION: Read the book (or select one from the Annotated Bibliography).
Prepare a chart with the heading: "We listen to our strong side when...".**

1. Introduce the activity by asking students what they think the phrase "listen to your strong side" means.

2. After a few students volunteer ideas, ask the class to think about the phrase while you read the story.

3. Read the book.

4. Start a discussion of the story by asking "How did JoJo listen to her strong side?"

5. Make a chart of students' answers to the question, "We listen to our strong side when... ."

6. Add to the chart over several days and then review it.

7. Plan a class activity to celebrate how students listened to their strong side, e.g., a special treat, an extra game period.

1-2 Activity: Poster campaign (3-4 class sessions)

MATERIALS NEEDED: Oaktag or other poster-making paper; markers

PREPARATION: Consider coordinating with other teachers about participating in a grade-wide or school-wide poster campaign that will highlight "Doing the Right Thing" when someone is in trouble.

1. Introduce the activity by asking students what it means to "Do the Right Thing" when you see that someone is being teased or bullied.

2. Ask students to share stories of times when they did help someone in trouble. Point out that everyone has a responsibility to try to do something about teasing or bullying behavior when they see it happening.

3. Suggest the idea of a poster campaign to let other classes in the school know how important it is to step in and help when you observe teasing or bullying or to stop bullying if you are the one doing it.

4. Have students decide whether they want to design a poster individually, in pairs, or working in cooperative small groups.

5. Talk about how to make an effective poster — bright colors, large print and/or drawing, neat work.

6. Plan with students how to set up a display of the posters that can be seen by the whole school.

7. Set aside ample class time for students to plan and create their posters.

2-3 Activity: Journal writing (1 class session)

MATERIALS NEEDED: Student journals

1. Introduce the phrase "Listen to your strong side," and ask students to share some ideas about what they think it means.

2. Ask, "Could it have something to do with courage?" Facilitate the discussion by helping students to talk about how it could take courage to help someone who is being teased or bullied.

3. Have students write in their journals about a time they "listened to their strong side."

4. Ask for volunteers to share what they wrote with the class.

2-3 Activity: Standing up for someone stories (1-2 class sessions)

MATERIALS NEEDED: Paper; pencils

1. Have students create individual or group stories about "standing up for someone."

2. Ask students to write about an incident of teasing that they witnessed (but without using real names). The story should answer three questions:

> What happened?
> What did you do about it?
> What did you wish you had done about it?

3. If students need help, suggest possible topics:

> Teasing that happens while walking to school
> Making fun of someone's intelligence or appearance
> Teasing on the school bus
> Making fun of someone's sports ability
> Excluding someone at lunch
> Playing pranks
> Spreading rumors
> Boys teasing girls
> Girls teasing boys

4. Have a read-aloud session to share the stories.

HOMEWORK **The creative-writing assignment can be given as homework, followed by class discussion.**

LESSON THREE:
BREAKING DOWN BARRIERS TO FRIENDSHIP

Students explore how teasing, bullying, and social attitudes can keep them from being friends.

K-2 Activity: Building and problem-solving (1 class session)

MATERIALS NEEDED: Wooden or large cardboard blocks; masking tape; chart paper; markers

PREPARATION: Before you begin this activity, be sure students understand the meaning of the word "barrier." Point out that barriers can be both physical (like the wall they're going to build) or attitudinal (like not playing with someone just because they're a girl or because they're a boy).

1. Ask students:

What kinds of things keep people from being friends?
What are some things we say or do that can harm friendship?

2. Make a list as students talk. Explain that you are going to build a wall with blocks. Demonstrate how the activity will work. Tell students, "Let's say it is Jo's turn (use a fictitious name) and Jo says, 'You can't play with us.' I will write that on the chart paper, and Jo will take a block and start the wall. We'll follow that process until everyone has had a turn.

3. Write down what each student says on chart paper and then have the student place her or his block on the wall. It doesn't matter if several students say the same thing, each one gets a turn to add a block.

4. Once the wall is built, ask half the class to sit on one side of the wall, and half the class on the other.

5. Explain that each time we do one of these things, we create a wall or barrier that keeps people from being friends.

6. Present the following problem:

You all want to be friends, but there is this big barrier in the way.
What can you do to take away each one of these blocks?

7. Each time a student comes up with a solution (e.g., make a rule that girls and boys can play together, no one can say you can't play, don't hurt people's feelings), have him or her remove the block. When taking down the wall, students can remove any block, not necessarily the one they put up.

8. Follow this activity with a group game, snack, or song to celebrate taking down the barrier.

ANECDOTE

One kindergarten teacher had students build a barrier wall around all the stuffed animals. The barrier stayed up all day, and then the students had to problem-solve about what to say to bring the barrier down.

2-3 Activity: Creative writing and performing (1-2 class sessions)

MATERIALS NEEDED: Index cards; writing materials

1. On index cards, give each student one of the situations from the following list of barriers to friendship.

> Someone won't let you and your friend join in a game on the playground.
> A boy answers a question in class, and some other kids start to laugh.
> Two kids are whispering. Then they point to you and start laughing.
> Someone tells you that your clothes are gross.
> Some boys won't let you shoot baskets. They yell, "You can't play, no girls allowed."
> Some girls are running relay races. When some boys want to join in they say,
>   "You can't play, no boys allowed."
> Someone teases you about your new glasses.

 TEACHER TIP

> **You can also use actual situations that you have seen occurring in your class/school or you can ask students to write about a situation that has happened to a friend or themselves.**

2. Ask students to write a poem or rap song about their situation. Students can work in pairs, small groups, or individually.

3. In creating their poems or songs, ask students to:

> **Consider how all the people are feeling**
> **Include courageous, non-violent ways to resolve the situation**

4. Have students read the poems or perform the songs for the class.

5. Extend the activity by having students perform and/or teach their poems and songs to younger students.

 Older students can read about the Berlin Wall — why it was constructed as a barrier, how it kept families apart, and how people actually took it down.

2-3 Activity: Writing friendship poems
(Introduction, plus 1 class session)

MATERIALS/PREPARATION: Make a copy of *The Friendship Poem* **worksheet for each student**

INTRODUCTION

Introduce the activity by asking students:

> What makes a good friend?
> Why are friends important?
> Do girls have boys as friends? Why? Why not?
> Do boys have girls as friends? Why? Why not?

Explain that they are going to be writing poems about friendship. You may want to read a poem as an example, and talk about some of the elements of poetry, e.g. rhyming cadence.

HOMEWORK **Give out The Friendship Poem worksheet as a homework assignment.**

1. After students have completed their poems, ask for volunteers to read theirs to the class.

2. Expand on the activity by compiling the poems into a book, holding a poetry reading with other classes in the school, or publishing the poems in a school newspaper.

Sample: Poems from a 3rd Grade

Friends are very special
If you have a friend you're not alone
Friends are important for me to have
If I did not have a friend
Who would I play with?
If I did not have a friend
Who would I talk to?
Friends are very special!

""" **Sample: Poems from a 3rd Grade**

Today someone teased me for the
color of my skin.
They called me dumb and had a
particular grin.
I said it didn't matter what my
religion or my race is.
I said I didn't care what the color
of my face is.
They said it was true.
So now we are friends
And that's how the whole story ends.

When you're down in the dumps
and bullies give you bumps
and you really need a friend...Wait! Here he comes!
He gives you a slap on the head.
You return a jab,
but before you know it you're bagged.
But you know it's just play.
No matter what you say.
You're best friends.

The Friendship Poem

Name: _____ Date:_____

We have talked about teasing and bullying, and all of you shared important feelings. We acted out different issues of teasing, and many of the situations involved the importance of listening to each other and trusting friends. We made a list of statements that will help people think and avoid conflicts.

Having a friend. Being a friend. Trusting a person. Respecting people are powerful emotional feelings.

Use the space below to create a poem about one of these feelings.

_____

_____

_____

_____

_____

_____

_____

_____

_____

Re-read your poem. Correct any errors. Does it express your thoughts?

Problem Solving

Puppet / role-plays / stop action stories

The following problem-solving scenarios help students practice thinking of realistic and non-violent ways to stand up for themselves or someone else. If students suggest an idea that is unrealistic or dangerous, guide them to think it through to its logical consequence with questions such as:

How do you think that might work out?

What are some of the pros and cons?

Do you think you might get hurt?

What else could you do that would be safer for you?

It is important for students to understand that there are ways to help someone without putting themselves in harm's way. The scenarios can be acted out with puppets, as role-plays, or stop-action stories, whichever works best for your class. (For instructions on using puppets, role-plays, or stop-action stories, please see section on Problem-Solving Techniques.)

K-1 Puppet or Role Play

Joanne and David are best friends. They want to sit together in the lunchroom, but all the girls sit at one table and all the boys at the other. When David sits with the girls, they call him, "Sissy." When Joanne sits with the boys, they tease her and call her "Joe."

1-2 Puppet or Role Play

On the school bus, a couple of fourth-grade girls have begun to tease a new girl, who came into the school late in the year. Every morning, the girls whisper and point as she gets on the bus. They pull her hair and then pretend they didn't. Two other fourth-grade girls are tired of watching this happen every day. They think it is mean to make a kid so uncomfortable.

1-2 Puppet or Role Play

Toby always does mean things to other kids when the teacher isn't looking, and all the other kids in the class know it. Some even egg Toby on or laugh when she trips up someone or takes their pencil and pretends she didn't. But a few other kids are tired of Toby's tricks and want to stand up to her and make her stop.

2-3 Stop-action Stories

✦ A fifth-grade bully waits outside of school and demands money from 4th graders who walk home from school.

✦ A group of kids run out from lunch before everyone else and grab all the jump ropes.

✦ A boy arrives in school from another country and doesn't know much English. Some kids laugh at his accent or when he mispronounces a word.

✦ A girl student is being teased that she has a boy friend.

✦ A boy student is being teased that he has a girl friend.

Literature Connections

K-3 Activity: Courage Is...?
Carlson, Nancy. *Arnie and the Skateboard Gang*. New York: Viking/Penguin, 1995.
Hoffman, Mary. *Amazing Grace*. New York: Dial Books for Young Readers, 1991.
Mohr, Nicholasa. *Felita*. New York: Bantam Skylark, 1990.

K-1 Activity: We listen to our strong side
Pinkney, Brian. *JoJo's Flying Side Kick*. New York: Simon & Schuster Books for Young Readers, 1995.

Additional Suggestions for Theme
Baum, Frank. *The Wizard of Oz*. New York: Holt, Rinehart & Winston, 1982 ed. (3, chapter)
Cohen, Barbara. *Molly's Pilgrim*. New York: William Morrow and Co., Inc., 1983.
    (2-3, easy reader)
Gogoll, Martine. *Rosie's Story*. Greenvale, NY: Mondo Publishing, 1994.
    (K-3, picture/easy reader).
Golenbock, Peter. *Teammates*. San Diego: Harcourt Brace Jovanovich, 1990.
    (2-3, picture/easy reader)

Connecting with Families

1. Send students' writings and drawings home each week in a special folder.

2. Invite families to an "opening" of the poster campaign display.

3. Invite families in to a performance of student poems and rap songs.

4. Use The Friendship Poem worksheet as an assignment to do at home with a family member.

Dear family member,

In our activities about teasing and bullying, we have been talking about courage and what it means to stand up for oneself or someone else. The class has agreed that teasing and bullying hurts feelings and that everyone has a responsibility to help stop it from happening, without using violence or putting themselves in danger.

Your child may ask you (or another family member) about a time when you stood up for someone who was being teased or bullied, or someone stood up for you. Please help your child draw, write, or even tape record about this experience. Children will be sharing their family stories with the class. You can help by asking your child questions such as:

> What do you think it means to "stand up for someone?"
> Did you ever stand up for someone who was being teased or bullied?
> Who was it? How did it happen?
> Were you afraid? Would you do it again?
> Did anyone ever stand up for you? Who was it?
> What did that person do?
> How did it make you feel?

With regards,

Physical Games
and Exercises

The guide takes the issue of teasing and bullying
"out of the moment," and provides students with language to
use in a discussion that is not charged with emotion.

– School Administrator

Physical activity is important to the well-being of everyone. Students, especially those in the early elementary grades, have a strong need to balance their sedentary learning tasks with frequent breaks for physical activity as a way of relaxing and reducing stress, relieving restlessness, and staying focused.

As adults who have learned relaxation techniques or who exercise after work can attest, these strategies help to ease the tensions of the typical day and to put stressful encounters with colleagues into perspective. Students, too, can benefit from learning similar techniques to cope with frustration, anger, and stress, which in turn can head off some teasing and bullying behavior before it begins.

Unfortunately, in many elementary schools, there is a decreasing emphasis on physical education. There are just not enough opportunities for young students to move, stretch, and exercise their bodies. Nor is there time for students to take a break for a quiet moment alone. Even short breaks of 5 to 10 minutes can be beneficial. Both the active movement and quieting exercises described in this section can be easily incorporated into the daily life of the classroom and can be shared with parents to do with their children at home.

It is also worth noting the kind of activity that students engage in outdoors during recess. Research has shown that recess in most schools is a time when large groups of students are released into a yard under the supervision of few adults. To make matters more difficult, these adults typically have little authority and often receive no training in group management. There is little or no equipment, and students have to struggle for control of the few balls or jump ropes that are available. As a result, the yard becomes an arena where much fighting, teasing, and bullying occur and where justice does not prevail.

Researchers have found that aggressive playground behavior of elementary school students is reduced when unstructured play or competitive games (i.e., where there is a winner or loser) are replaced by organized noncompetitive games.[1] In Play Fair, a program developed at the Rhode Island Department of Education's Office of Special Needs, an area of the playground is sectioned off and designated for noncompetitive games. As a result, bullying behavior between students decreased significantly both on the playground and in the classroom.[2]

The activities in this section are meant to be used informally and as needed during the school day. Students, individually and in groups, can engage in moving, stretching, and breathing activities.

- If you feel tensions rising or if students have had a stressful activity such as a test, conduct one of the Deep Breathing, Muscle Relaxation, or Yoga exercises.
- If students have difficulty during transition times, use one of the Movement Games to help them focus.
- If students need a place to escape peer pressure, calm down, or just collect their thoughts, set up a Safe Haven — a designated quiet area — in the classroom. At first, you may need to suggest to students that they retreat to the quiet area, but over time the goal for students will be able to decide independently when to use the Safe Haven to regain their equilibrium.

• If a student is angry, help him or her cool off with a Calming Exercise. This is especially important in the context of teasing and bullying. It is very helpful for students to learn specific ways to cool off when they might feel like taking it out on someone else.

• If recess is becoming a time when teasing and bullying behavior is escalating, set up an area where students can play Tag with a Purpose, and train a parent or aide to oversee it. You may want to talk to the administration of the school about re-thinking supervision or grouping of students during recess and providing sport equipment or structured noncompetitive games.

It is important to remember that all people — children and adults — have varying degrees of comfort with their bodies and in relation to different types of physical activities. Students should be encouraged to adapt any physical activity to their levels of comfort and abilities. No student should be made to do an activity if she or he is uncomfortable about it. This can also help students who have been frightened by or discouraged from participating in physical activities realize that they can succeed if they take things at their own speed.

K-3 Calming Exercises

QUIETING SOUNDS

1. Select one of the following quieting sound effects and "play it" for students to create a listening mood.

Sound one note from a xylophone. For variety, try a different pitch or volume and ask students how that changes their mood. You can change the note daily, weekly or periodically to see if students notice. If not, ask them, "Did anyone notice something different about the chime?" Play the former sound and the new sound for them.

Wrap two blocks in fine gauge sandpaper and rub them together. Quietly and slowly tap a wood block and knocker (from a set a rhythm instruments) or use rhythmic clapping patterns with students. Pour water (or sand) from one container to another, or pour water through a strainer into a bucket to create a rain sound.

Shake a rainstick. Sound a windchime.

2. Pause for a moment for quiet to take effect. Ask students, "If this sound was a color, what would it be?" Ask them to close their eyes and imagine what this sound would look like. What did they see?

3. Ask students if they can think of other quieting (or calming) sounds they would like to add to the classroom collection.

SAFE HAVEN

1. Set up quiet areas in the classroom where one or two students can "retreat" when feeling stressed (e.g., a reading corner, a rocker, a beanbag chair, a study carrel).

2. Provide soothing activities in these areas, for example, portable tape player with head phones, koosh or squish balls, play dough or clay to squeeze, fish tank, kaleidoscopes, "ocean" bottles, etc.

3. Keep the "quieting sounds" equipment on a shelf where students can reach them. Students can select one of the sound effects to use when they feel a need to quiet things down, or when you as teacher request that they do so.

DEEP BREATHING

1. Ask students to form a circle and sit with their legs crossed. Or, if they find it more comfortable, they can sit back on their heels. In either position, it is important to tell students to sit up tall, so that their backs are straight.

2. Use one of the quieting sounds. Ask students to breathe in as deeply as they can when the sound begins, and then let the breath out slowly until the sound ends. Have them practice; each time you can make the sound last a little longer. Repeat about three times, until everyone seems calm and focused.

3. Explain that students can go to a quiet corner and do deep breathing when they are feeling stressed during the school day.

MUSCLE RELAXATION

1. Introduce students to the relaxation technique of tightening and relaxing their muscles. Tell students to take a deep breath: As they do this, ask them to concentrate and tighten their shoulders and pull them up as high as they can toward their ears.

2. Then, together, count to six, and have students let out their breath and slowly bring their shoulders down.

3. Rest a few seconds and repeat by tightening and relaxing different parts of the body. Students can do this exercise while sitting in their seats, taking a very short break from their work.

4. You may want to have students stretch out on the floor when tightening and relaxing their legs, feet, arms, and hands. Be sure to take into account students' different developmental levels of muscle control.

VISUALIZATION AND COUNTING

1. Have each student think of a pleasant scene that he or she would find calming. It might be a beach or a mountain that was visited during vacation, or it might be a pure fantasy. Assure students that the choice is theirs.

2. Ask students to think of their chosen scene and then count to 25 slowly. Practice the exercise a few times with the whole class and then add it to the roster of calming activities that students can use to relieve tension as a group or individually during the school day.

K-3 Movement Games

GET UP AND MOVE

1. Several times during the school day, especially during transitions, gather the students together for some simple movement games:

Signal and response: Decide on a specific movement that students will do when they hear you clap your hands (e.g., jumping in place) and another when you stomp your feet (e.g., making circles with their arms). The game can be made more challenging for older students by adding a number of different signals and responses.

Arm circles: Have students make big circles with their arms, one going forward, the other back. Ask students to follow directions with their eyes closed.

A leg to stand on: Have students try different movements while standing on one leg.

Follow the leader: Ask one student to imitate the pose of an animal or plant, and then have all the others try to pose the same way.

Creative movement: Have students create movement to music.

YOGA TECHNIQUES

1. Spend some time exploring yoga movements that help students relax, concentrate, and be still. Many yoga positions are named for animals; have students make up games using the characteristic of each animal.

Dog: Start on all fours with palms of hands and knees on the floor. Breathe in, tuck toes under. Breathe out and lift up hips, slowly straightening out your legs. Stretch so arms and legs are straight. Bend knees, sit gently on heels, bend forward and relax.

Cat: Start on all fours with palms of hands and knees on the floor. Breathe in, hollow back keeping arms straight and shoulders relaxed. Breathe out, arching back in opposite direction. Come back to original position.

Snake: Lie flat, face down, with hands beside chest. Keep palms down and fingers pointing forwards. Breathe in, then breathe out and, keeping very flat on the floor, slide forwards lifting head and chest off the floor.

SPACE SCULPTURES

1. Divide the class into two groups, standing at opposite ends of the room (or yard).

2. Begin by asking students in group one to form a bridge (or a tunnel), which the other students go under (or through) without touching anyone. Have each group take turns being the structure.

3. When students are comfortable with the bridge and tunnel structures, ask them to make a "sculpture" by connecting their arms or legs as well as their hands. They can twist their bodies, spread their legs wide apart, lift one leg, connect legs to legs, legs to arms, etc. When group one has made their sculpture, they shout, "ready," and group two runs through the spaces in the sculpture without touching anyone. Then the groups exchange roles and repeat the activity.

➤ **T E A C H E R   T I P :**

> Students will feel most comfortable playing this game if they know and feel safe with one another.

TAG WITH A PURPOSE

1. In these versions of tag, the focus is shifted away from "being chased." It is central to all of these games that players are never "out." Either their roles change or they can be released back into the game by other players. Sometimes players are on their own in dodging and running to safety; at other times, they are helped by one or more people.

2. Before going outside to play, talk about how students feel when playing a game of tag. Do they like to be chased? Do they like to do the chasing? How does it feel to be tagged out? Get their ideas about other ways the game might be played. Then, tell them that they are going to be playing different kinds of tag — ones where nobody is ever "out."

> **Sparrows in the Trees:** Starts with one student being the "tagger." She/he stands in the middle of the yard/room/gym. As the other players (the "sparrows") run from one end of the playing area to the other, the tagger tries to touch them. If they are tagged, they become "trees." They cannot move their feet, but they can tag the other players if they come close. When there are only one or two runners left, the tagger also becomes a tree. When only a few sparrows are left, it is important to give them the option of continuing to run or not. Some students love the challenge of having to go around everyone, but some can feel intimidated.

Stop and Go: A number of students begin as "taggers;" a few others have gloves. Once a student is tagged (on the shoulder), then she or he is "frozen." When someone who is frozen yells, "help," another student can pass them a glove which "unfreezes" them. The number of taggers and gloves depends on the number of players and the size of the playing area.

Circle of Friends: A number of students begin as "taggers" and can freeze other students by tagging them on the shoulder. In this version, if a frozen student calls for help, two students hold hands and form a circle around her/him. This circle of friends unfreezes the student so he or she can continue playing. Students can't be tagged while making a circle.

➤ TEACHER TIP:

Having a clear beginning, end, and/or pause time built into the game helps maintain the structure, allows for more adult supervision of the game's movement and energy, and provides for a check-in time if students become overstimulated.

3. Once back in the classroom, use an activity from Quieting Sounds or Stress Relief to help the transition from active play to focused work.

[1] R. Slaby, W. Roedell, D. Arezzo, and K. Hendrix, *Early Violence Prevention: Tools for Teachers of Young Children* (Washington, D.C.: National Association for the Education of Young Children, 1995).

[2] M. Chuoke and B. Eyman, "Play Fair–and Not Just at Recess," *Educational Leadership* (Vol. 54, No. 8), 1997.

This section is based on the work of the Children's Empowerment Project of the Center for Anti-Violence Education in Brooklyn, New York.

Problem-Solving Techniques

It is typically the most shy, the smallest, the quietest

children who are recipients of teasing and bullying.

When I implemented the role-playing activity from the guide,

and those students assumed the role of bystander,

they became more vocal and stood up for others.

– Third-grade teacher

Unless students themselves take an active role, teasing and bullying are likely to continue whenever an adult is not there to intervene. Student actions can take several forms: 1) eliminating (or lessening) their own teasing/bullying behavior; 2) stopping someone from teasing or bullying them; and 3) learning how to intervene as a bystander.

Students often lack the language and social problem-solving strategies to eliminate teasing and bullying on their own. They need adults to model positive problem-solving techniques (words and actions), to provide direct support for their efforts, and to respond with appropriate and effective consequences when their efforts are not completely successful in stopping the teasing and bullying.

Most important, however, students need numerous opportunities to practice in a safe environment and to assess the pros and cons of different approaches. The approaches students choose will depend on many factors — age, size, gender, temperament, popularity, etc.

This section describes a variety of techniques to help students learn to problem-solve. These various approaches help students try out specific words and actions and provide a reference point for them when they are confronted with real-life teasing and bullying situations. In order to create a non-threatening environment for students to practice in, you will need to establish guidelines for setting a tone of trust and respect in the classroom.

The following techniques are described in this section:

- Using books to highlight key points;
- Using puppets to dramatize scenarios;
- Doing role-plays to practice various problem-solving solutions;
- Employing stop-action stories that break at critical points for discussion and problem-solving; and
- Reading and discussing vignettes to stimulate thinking and problem-solving.

Select the technique that you feel is most developmentally-appropriate for your students. For example, using puppets is a good device for younger students, while slighter older students can try simple role-plays. Stop-action stories might be most effective with older students. Books and vignettes can be used across grade levels.

Sample problem-solving scenarios and vignettes are included within each theme in this Guide. We encourage you to adapt them or to invent your own using real-life examples from student writing and drawings, class discussions, and your own observations.

Books

Children's literature provides many opportunities to talk about ways of handling conflicts and can be particularly helpful in facilitating students' discussions about teasing and bullying — e.g., what the conflict is about; how the characters are feeling; or what motivates them. It also provides students with an opportunity to predict how the characters might handle a situation and then evaluate the character's response — e.g., whether the solution was successful; how they might have handled things differently.

Books also provide a good resource for role-playing. Students can act out a story or scene, or they can use puppets to act out the story line. Students can be encouraged to create their own books or to create new endings for the stories you read.

1. Select a book where the character is faced with a problem or conflict about teasing and bullying. (See Annotated Bibliography for a description of a wide range of books for grades K-3. Books are also suggested within each theme as well as within particular activities.)

2. Read the book up to the point of conflict.

3. Ask students:
How are the characters feeling?
What do you think the conflict is about?
Can you think of ways the characters could solve their problem?
Which solution do you think the characters will use?

4. Finish reading the story, and then ask:
How did the characters resolve the conflict?
Do you think it was a good solution? Why or why not?
How do the characters feel now?

Puppets

Puppets can provide a novel way to engage students in problem-solving. You can use puppets to act out scenes in conjunction with books or role-play scenarios to illustrate various problem-solving solutions and consequences. Using puppets as an effective tool may take some practice so that you will not feel self-conscious in front of students. Feel free to create voices and personalities for each puppet you use.

Simple puppets hold students' attention without distracting them from the content. Foam bath puppets are inexpensive and easy to use, and there also are a number of easy ways to make your own:

Use popsicle sticks or tongue depressors (available from craft stores and catalogs), markers, and glue. You also can add bits of fabric to suggest clothing, but it is not essential.

Use a paper bag and a dowel. With a sandwich size bag, draw a face, stuff the bag with shredded newspaper, place a dowel in the bag and secure the bottom of the bag with a rubber band.

Use a sock, drawing a face with markers.

> **TEACHER TIP:**

> **As an alternative, you can improvise by using small dolls or stuffed animals in place of puppets.**

1. Using the puppets, act out one scenario for the class. Limit the puppet scene to one to-two minutes until students are comfortable with the activity.

2. Use the puppets to act out the problem up until the point of conflict. You can show the problem escalating, but don't let the puppets hit, punch, or fight. Instead, simply tell what happened next or stop the scene at this point.

3. After you have acted out the scene, ask students what they think the puppets should do. Encourage them to address the puppets directly — and have the puppets respond to them directly. Ask:

> **What do you think is happening here? What is the problem?**
> **How are the puppets feeling? Can you show us how they are feeling?**
> **What should the puppets do next? Tell them what you would like them to do.**
> **Have you ever had a problem like this one?**
> **What could the puppets do to keep this problem from happening again?**

4. Don't censor students' responses — acknowledge them and have the puppets explore the potential consequences.

Role-Plays

Acting out roles for themselves is an excellent way to help students problem-solve ways to resolve teasing and bullying conflicts. As noted earlier, you will find sample scenarios within each theme in this Guide. However, creating role-plays drawn from student writing and drawing, class discussion, and your own observations will make them more relevant for your students.

1. Choose students (or ask students to volunteer) to role-play one of the skits.

> **TEACHER TIP:**

> **If you are assigning roles, be sure not to have the boys always in the role of the aggressor/initiator.**

2. Explain that role-playing is just what it says: it's playing a role, or a part, just like in a play. And it gives students the opportunity to put themselves "in someone else's shoes."

3. When doing the role-play, be sure to stop at the moment of conflict and ask for students' suggestions about what the actors should do.

4. Follow up with questions that lead students to reflect on the feelings involved. Ask:
> **How do you think the teaser/bully (the initiator) felt?**
> **How do you think the person being teased/bullied (the recipient) felt?**
> **How do you think the people watching (the bystanders) felt?**
> **Did the bystanders "stand up for someone?" Should they? What could they do?**

5. Ask students what the characteristics of the teasers and bullyers were in the role-play:

Did they make any facial expressions?

Did they stand a particular way?

Did they use kind language?

Were they following the classroom rules?

What were the students like who were being teased and bullied?

How did they look? act? move?

Were there any bystanders?

What were the bystanders doing? How do you think they felt? What could they have done?

6. Discuss pros and cons of possible solutions:

Ignoring the teaser

Walking away

Using words like "stop," "stay away"

Asking a friend to help

Asking for help from an adult

Diverting the bully's attention

Distracting the bully with humor

Trying to reason or compromise

Stop-Action Stories

With this technique, students pretend they are making a video to tell or act out a teasing or bullying story line up to the point of conflict or confrontation. The action is then stopped, and the "audience" is asked to provide alternative solutions. They continue the story to the logical resolution — or next point of conflict. Students can also work in production groups to create video "story boards." They can make and use props such as cameras, "cut" boards, "mikes," and scenery. Either way, stop-action stories provide a fun way to practice real-life situations.

1. You can have students develop teasing and bullying story lines from books, from incidents they have observed, from their own personal experiences, or you can use the story lines suggested in the themes throughout the Guide.

2. Students act out the story in the following way:
> During the "action" part of the video, they act the story to the point of conflict.
> Then they stop or "freeze" and yell, "cut."
> The audience comes up with solutions.
> The players then act out one (or several) of these to their conclusion(s).

➤ **TEACHER TIP:**

> **Stress that at no point should students even mime aggressive actions. They can say it, but not act it out.**

Vignettes

Vignettes provide realistic stories with teasing and bullying dilemmas for students to problem-solve. Each vignette includes questions to stimulate students' thinking.

1. Give a group of three-to-four students a copy of a vignette to read and discuss.

2. Bring the groups together, and ask students to read the vignette and to present their solutions.

3. Follow up with a discussion of their responses. Ask:
> What solution do you think makes the most sense? Why?
> Has anything like this ever happened to you?
> How did you handle it?
> What would you do if it happened again?

4. For younger students, read the vignette aloud and answer questions as a group.

➤ **TEACHER TIP:**

> **Be sure to set ground rules for discussion. For example: everyone will have a chance to talk; when someone else is talking, the rest of us will be quiet and listen; if you share a personal experience don't use real names. Also, use only one or two vignettes at a time, so students will have adequate opportunies to discuss and compare their responses.**

Annotated Bibliography

The Guide provides teachers, children, and parents with a safe way to talk about teasing and bullying; in a sense it gives them permission to talk about it.

For example, a child who was a school applicant was sitting in my office and clearly reading the "teasing & bullying" poster I had on my wall.

He said to me, "I'm not, but I know people who are!"

– School Administrator

OVERVIEW

Books are an important resource for addressing the issue of teasing and bullying in school and at home. Through books, students learn that they are not alone in experiencing teasing and bullying, and that others have thought of solutions that they might apply to their own particular situations. Books can also serve as a catalyst to spur students' self-expression through writing about teasing and bullying. There are several things to keep in mind when selecting books on this issue:

- Opt for good literature with interesting illustrations.
- Look for books that don't stereotype boys and girls, i.e., don't always present boys as bullies and aggressors and girls as victims. Also, be somewhat wary of books published before 1970. While some may be classics, other perpetuate narrow stereotypic roles for women and girls and men and boys.
- Choose books that use dialogues, situations, and strategies that are realistic representations of how your students talk and act. Avoid those that use magic or unreal solutions, e.g magic talismans or problem-solvers from outer space.
- Look for books that promote age-appropriate and realistic solutions to teasing and bullying problems. Avoid books where the bully gets a "taste of his/her own medicine" or where the bully is befriended by the victim and they live happily changed lives.

Be sure to read books from cover to cover before sharing them with students. Whenever possible, avoid using books with the flaws listed above. If, however, you find you need to choose one of these flawed books for a particular situation, use it as a point of discussion. Problem-solve with students about what would have been a better or more realistic approach/solution.

BOOKS FOR STUDENTS

Asch, Frank and Vladimir Vagin. *Here Comes the Cat!*
New York: Scholastic, 1989. ISBN# 0-59041-854-8   GR K-1 (P) [Barriers]
   A community of mice is gripped with fear when they learn that a cat is coming.
But they find their prejudice and fear are unfounded when they discover the cat has come in peace and friendship. This story provides opportunities to talk with younger children about prejudice and what can change attitudes.

Baum, Frank. *The Wizard of Oz*. New York: Holt, Rinehart & Winston, 1982 ed.
ISBN# 0-03061-661-1 GR3 (C)   [Courage; Problem-Solving Teasing & Bullying]
   This well-known story about Dorothy and her adventures in the Emerald City with the Lion, Scarecrow, and Tin Man provides opportunities to talk about different kinds of courage and the strategies bullies use to gain power over others and undermine their courage.

Blume, Judy. *Iggie' s House*. New York: Dell Publishing Co., Inc., 1970.
ISBN# 0-4440-44062-9   GR 3 (C) [Problem-Solving Teasing & Bullying; Barriers]
   When a black family with three children moves into the white neighborhood, eleven-year-

---

KEY: (P) = picture book (ER) = easy reader (C) =chapter book   (V) = video
GR = approximate grade level [Courage; Barriers] = themes, lessons, issues

old Winnie learns the difference between being a good neighbor and being a good friend.

Bosch, Carl W. *Bully on the Bus*. Seattle, WA: Parenting Press, Inc., 1988.
ISBN# 0-943990-42-4 GR 3 (ER) [Problem-Solving Teasing & Bullying]
  A big fifth grade boy on the school bus has been picking on you — what will you do? Part of the Decision is Yours series, this book allows students to choose a variety of realistic ways of responding to a typical bullying problem — and depict likely outcomes of each. While this book focuses on boy characters, it might be an interesting addition to your free reading bookshelf.

Brown, Marc. *Arthur's April Fool*. Boston: Little Brown, 1983.
ISBN# 0-31611-1961 GR K-2 (P) [Problem-Solving Teasing & Bullying]
  Arthur's worries about remembering his magic tricks for the class assembly are compounded by threats by Binky, the class bully, to pulverize him. (Also available on audio cassette.)

Caple, Kathy. *The Wimp*. Boston: Houghton Mifflin, 1994.
ISBN# 0-39563-1157 GR 1-3 (P) [Problem-Solving Teasing & Bullying]
  Arnold the pig and his sister Rose give two bullies a taste of their own medicine when Arnold decides he doesn't want to be called a wimp anymore. This book has a rather simplistic ending, but it is good for problem-solving and provides an opportunity to talk about courage. It also demonstrates how words such as wimp or sissy are used and the gender stereotypes they project.

Carle, Eric. *The Grouchy Ladybug*. New York: Scholastic Book Services, 1977.
ISBN# 0-59031-2278 GR K (P) [Problem-Solving Teasing & Bullying]
  A grouchy ladybug is looking for a fight and challenges everyone she meets regardless of their size or strength.

Carlson, Nancy. *Arnie and the Skateboard Gang*. New York: Viking/Penguin, 1995.
ISBN# 0-670-85722-x GR 2-3 (P) [Problem-Solving Teasing & Bullying; Courage; Peer Pressure]
  When the Fly challenges Arnie to skateboard down a dangerous hill, he has to decide how far he's willing to go to be cool. The author uses colorful, cartoon-like animal characters to illustrate this book about peer pressure and courage. When Arnie does not give in to peer pressure, other characters are grateful to him, and he has the courage to say no to a perilous act. While the text and illustrations may be appealing to younger children, the discussion about peer pressure and who is courageous will be more meaningful with second and third graders.

Carlson, Nancy. *How to Lose All Your Friends*. New York: Puffin/Penguin Books, 1994.
ISBN# 0-140-55862-4 GR K-3 (P) [Friendship; Problem-Solving Teasing & Bullying]
  With tongue-in-cheek humor, this book offers advice on all the things you can do if you don't want to have any friends. It provides an opportunity to talk about behaviors that can make children feel unwelcome or uncomfortable, and also may provide a starting point to talk about social rules concerning how to get along and treat each other.

Carlson, Nancy. *Loudmouth George and the Sixth Grade Bully*. New York: Puffin Books, 1985. ISBN# 0-140-50510-5 GR 1-2 (P) [Problem-Solving Teasing & Bullying]
  This book tells the story of Loudmouth George (a rabbit) and his friend Harriet. When George has his lunch repeatedly stolen by a sixth grader twice his size, he is a hungry, nervous wreck. While this book is flawed, in that George and Harriet retaliate by preparing a

nasty decoy lunch for the bully, it provides an opportunity to discuss how it feels to be bullied, and generates an interesting discussion about the pros and cons of George's approach and what other strategies he might have used instead.

Carroll, Lewis. *Alice's Adventures in Wonderland.* New York: St. Martin's Press, 1976 ed. ISBN# 0-856-70-189-0   GR 2-3(C)   [Rules]
   Sections of this book, such as the queen's croquet match and the tea party, can be read aloud and used to illustrate what happens when rules are arbitrary or don't make sense.

Cohen, Barbara. *Molly's Pilgrim.* New York: William Morrow and Co., Inc., 1983. ISBN# 0-553-15833-3 GR 2-3 (ER) [Barriers; Problem Solving Teasing & Bullying]
   Molly is a Russian Jewish immigrant girl living in a small American town in the early part of the twentieth century. She hates her new school because her third grade classmates exclude her from their play and tease her about her accent, clothing, and foreign ways. When the teacher assigns a project to make a doll for a Thanksgiving unit, Molly's mother helps and — much to Molly's embarrassment — creates a doll that looks like a Russian peasant. This book provides opportunities to discuss barriers as well as teasing and bullying.

Cole, Joanna. *Bully Trouble.* New York: Random House, 1989. ISBN# 0-39484-9493 GR 3-4 (ER) [Problem-Solving Teasing & Bullying]
   When teased and bullied every day by an older boy, Arlo and Robby work together to try to stop him. This book is flawed in terms of the solution the boys come up with (they make an extra spicy decoy lunch for the bully to steal) and the outcome (the bully sees the error of his ways and reforms). However, it provides a nice build-up of how the recipient feels and provides a good springboard for discussion about possible solutions to teasing and bullying problems and potential consequences.

Cosby, Bill. *The Meanest Thing to Say.* New York: Scholastic, 1997. ISBN#: 0-590-95616-7   GR K-3 (P/ER) [Problem-Solving Teasing & Bullying]
   When a new boy tries to involve Little Bill and his second grade classmates in a game where they try to say the meanest thing possible to each other, Little Bill takes some advice from his dad on how to handle the situation. When Little Bill manipulates the confrontation without being mean himself, the bully's taunts fall flat, and he retreats in embarrassment. While these tactics and the outcome may not always be practical or realistic, the story provides an opportunity to discuss how words can be used to tease and bully, how games like these can cross the line from fun to hurtful, and ways of resolving conflicts without losing face or retaliating in kind.

Crary, Elizabeth. *My Name is Not Dummy.* Seattle: Parenting Press, 1983. ISBN# 0-9602862-8-4   GR K-2 (P)   [Problem-Solving Teasing & Bullying]
   Part of Elizabeth Crary's problem-solving series, this book focuses on teasing from the perspective of a child with cognitive delays. While it is rather didactic, it provides structure for talking about this issue with young students.

dePaola, Tomie. *Oliver Button is a Sissy.* San Diego: Voyager/Harcourt Brace Jovanovich, 1979. ISBN# 0-15-668140-4   GR K-2 (P) [Gender Issues; Problem-Solving Teasing & Bullying]
   Oliver is teased by the other boys because he is different. Eventually, their lives are enriched

KEY: (P) = picture book (ER) = easy reader (C) =chapter book (V) = video
GR = approximate grade level [Courage; Barriers] = themes, lessons, issues

when they learn to appreciate his differences. This book provides opportunities to discuss gender stereotypes and put-downs.

Estes, Elinor. *The Hundred Dresses*. San Diego: Voyager/Harcourt Brace Jovanovich,1972. ISBN# 0-15-642350-2 GR 3 (ER/C) [Problem-Solving Teasing & Bullying; Barriers; Courage]
 A group of girls pick on a new girl who comes from an economically struggling immigrant family from Eastern Europe. Told from the perspective of the bully's best friend, who gives into peer pressure and joins the crowd, this story has an uncomfortable ending that is sure to generate discussion about the role of bystanders and the consequences that "harmless" teasing can have on others. While, on the surface, some aspects of this book may appear to be dated, the story is timeless, and it provides opportunities to discuss gender and cultural stereotypes and how bullying can focus on class differences.

Gogoll, Martine. *Rosie's Story*. Greenvale, N Y: Mondo Publishing, 1994.
ISBN# 1-879531-62-3 GR K-3 (P/ER) [Problem-Solving Teasing & Bullying]
 Rosie is teased constantly because of her red hair and freckles. She is miserable at school and shows symptoms of stress. Finally, as part of a class assignment, Molly writes a story about Rusty, a boy who is similarly teased. This opens up a class discussion about feelings, empathy, and the harm of teasing.

Golenbock, Peter. *Teammates*. San Diego: Harcourt Brace Jovanovich, 1990.
ISBN# 0-15-2842-86-1   GR 2-3 (P/ER) [Barriers; Courage]
 This book tells the true story of baseball great Jackie Robinson, the first African-American to play Major League baseball, and his white teammate PeeWee Reese. Both men show tremendous courage in response to racial discrimination.

Henkes, Kevin. *Crysanthemum*. New York: Greenwillow Books, 1991.
ISBN# 0-688-09699-9   GR K-2 (P) [Problem-Solving Teasing & Bullying]
 Crysanthemum, a mouse, loves her name until she starts school and other children start making fun of it. This book, with it's humorous drawings, provides opportunities to discuss how it feels to be teased — especially about something we can't change about ourselves, and also demonstrates how teasing can be contagious and how sometimes adults don't help.

Hoban, Russell and Lillian Hoban. *A Bargain for Frances*. New York: Scholastic Book Services, 1970. ISBN# 0-5900-9291-X GR 1-2 (ER) [Problem-Solving Teasing & Bullying; Friendship]
 Frances foils Thelma's plot to trick her out of a new china set. For very young children, this provides an opportunity to talk about true friends and those who use bribes to make and keep friends.

Hoffman, Mary. *Amazing Grace*. New York: Dial Books for Young Readers, 1991.
ISBN# 0-80371-040-2   GR 1-2 (P/ER) [Barriers; Courage]
 When Grace learns that her class will be performing the play Peter Pan, she decides she wants to play the part of Peter. But everyone teases her and tells her she can't play Peter because she's a girl and because she's black. This book provides opportunities to talk about gender and how all kinds of stereotypes limit people, and about how standing up for what you believe in can take courage and perseverance.

Jones, Rebecca C. *Matthew and Tilly*. New York: Dutton Children's Books, 1991.
ISBN# 0-52-544-684-2   GR K-1 (P) [Problem-Solving Teasing & Bullying]
  Matthew and Tilly are good friends — most of the time. But sometimes they get sick of each other. When that happens, conflicts erupt, and things they each say and do make the conflicts escalate. This book provides opportunities to look at how words can hurt, and how conflicts can be made — and resolved successfully.

King-Smith, Dick. *Babe the Gallant Pig*. New York: Bullseye/Random House, 1995.
ISBN# 0-679-87393-7   GR 3+ (C) [Courage; Problem-Solving Teasing & Bullying; Barriers]
  When Babe, a young piglet, arrives at Hogget's farm, he has many obstacles to overcome. Through courage and determination, Babe demonstrates that where there's a will there's a way, with a little help from friends, of course. This book, which can be read aloud to second graders, provides numerous opportunities to talk about teasing and bullying behavior, being different, and the courage it takes to stand up for yourself, those you care about, and what you believe in.

Kraus, Robert. *Leo the Late Bloomer.* New York: Scholastic, 1971.
ISBN# 0-590622-706   GR K (P) [Problem-Solving Teasing & Bullying; Friends]
  While his peers can already write, draw, speak, read, and eat neatly, Leo the tiger is still waiting to "bloom." Although Leo is not teased about the ways he is different, this book provides opportunities to talk about how individuals are unique and about the kind of teasing that can occur when children are not able to do things at the same level as their peers.

Lalli, Judy. *Make Someone Smile and 40 More Ways to Be a Peaceful Person.*
Minneapolis, MN: Free Spirit Publishing, Inc., 1996.
ISBN# 0-915793-99-7   GR K-2 (P) [Friendship; Barriers]
  This book of photographs has very little text. Photographs portray diverse elementary school children interacting in positive and prosocial ways. The only reservation is that, while the second half shows boys and girls together (solving problems, singing, and enjoying each other's company), the photos in the first half of the book are separated by gender (i.e. all boys on some pages and all girls on others). However, this provides an opportunity to talk about how gender can sometimes be a barrier to getting along.

Lionni, Leo. *It's Mine!* New York: Alfred A. Knopf, 1986.
ISBN# 0-394-87-000-x   GR K-1 (P) [Problem-Solving Teasing & Bullying]
  Three frogs are in continual conflict over who owns the pond until a storm makes them understand the benefits of sharing. This book provides opportunities for students to act out different points of view in problem-solving conflicts.

Lionni, Leo. *Frederick*. New York: Scholastic, 1989.
ISBN# 0-3949-1040-0 (library binding) GR K-1 (P) [Barriers]
This is a story about a mouse whose insistence on being different causes resentment in his community — until they discover the value of his gifts.

Lionni, Leo. *Swimmy*. New York: Scholastic, 1989.
ISBN# 0-590430-491 GR K-1 (P) [Barriers; Problem Solving Teasing & Bullying]
  Swimmy is different. He stands out in his school of little fish. But he turns his difference

into an asset when he organizes the little fish to resolve their conflict with the big fish who preys on them.

Little, Jean. *Jess Was the Brave One.* Toronto: Viking, 1991.
ISBN# 0-670834-955   GR K-1 (P) [Courage; Problem-Solving Teasing & Bullying]
 This book tells the story of two sisters — Jess, the outgoing and brave one, and Claire, the timid, imaginative one. When Jess' favorite teddy bear is taken by a group of bigger kids, it is Claire who stands up to them. This book provides opportunities to talk about courage and ways of being creative and assertive (rather than aggressive) in trying to resolve teasing and bullying problems.

Mauser, Pat Rhoads. *A Bundle of Sticks*. New York: Atheneum, 1982.
ISBN# 0-68930-899-X   GR 3 (C) [Problem-Solving Teasing & Bullying]
 Boyd, a fifth grader, is at the mercy of Ben, the class bully. His parents disagree about what he should do — his father wants him to defend himself; his mother doesn't want him to learn to fight. He finally learns martial arts techniques (Kajukenbo) that teach him both ways to defend himself and a philosophy that allows him not to fight. This book is interesting because it explores different notions about what it means to defend yourself: If you learn to fight, will the bullying stop? Does it mean you have to fight? Does learning how to fight mean you always have to fight — or that you might like to?

Mohr, Nicholasa. *Felita.* New York: Bantam Skylark, 1990.
ISBN# 0-1553-157-922   GR 3 (C) [Barriers; Courage]
 When 8-year-old Felita and her family move from their tight-knit urban Hispanic community to a safer neighborhood, Felita is teased and shunned by her classmates. When the entire family faces discrimination, they decide to move back to their old neighborhood. This book provides opportunities to talk not only about exclusion and discrimination, but also about gender and courage. The dialogue contains many words in Spanish.

Naylor, Phyllis Reynolds. *King of the Playground.* New York: Atheneum, 1991.
ISBN# 0-689-31558-9   GR K-1 (P) [Barriers; Problem-Solving Teasing & Bullying]
 Kevin's dad helps him to think of alternatives to dealing with threats from a bossy peer. The two learn to play together by being assertive and thinking of positive alternatives to power strategies.

Paterson, Katherine. *Flip-flop Girl*. New York: Puffin Books, 1994.
ISBN# 0-140-37679-8 GR 3+ (C) [Barriers; Courage]
 Following the death of their father from cancer, 9-year-old Vinnie and her 5-year-old brother, Mason, move with their mother to a new town. While the two siblings try to cope with the upheaval in their lives in unique ways, Vinnie finds herself alternately embarrassed by and protective of her brother, who is the subject of teasing and ridicule because he is unable to speak. With the help and friendship of Lupe, also an outcast, the children learn about courage and the negative effects of stereotypes. This book provides opportunities to talk about differences, exclusion (particularly due to class differences), and what it feels like to have to defend someone you care about.

Pete, Bill. *Big Bad Bruce*. New York: Scholastic, 1977.
ISBN# 0-3953-2922-1 GR 2-4 (P) [Problem-Solving Teasing & Bullying]
 Bruce the bear is a bully. He finally meets his match when he meets the witch, who shrinks

him and gives him a taste of his own medicine. While the solution in this book is unrealistic and rather drastic, the book offers a humorous way to initiate a discussion about how teasing and bullying make others feel as well as advantages and disadvantages of possible solutions.

Petty, Kate and Charlotte Firmin. *Being Bullied*. Hauppauge, NY: Barron's, 1991
ISBN# 0-8120-4661-7 GR K-1 (P) [Problem-Solving Teasing & Bullying]
When Rita is bullied by Bella, another girl at school, she feels frustrated, sad, and scared until she finds a way to stand up to her. This book emphasizes the importance of telling an adult and also models some simple strategies children can use. The illustrations also provide a springboard to talk about different roles that bystanders can take in helping or hindering bullying behavior.

Pinkney, Brian. *JoJo's Flying Side Kick*. New York: Simon & Schuster Books for Young Readers, 1995. ISBN# 0-698-80283-8 GR 1-2 (P) [Courage]
JoJo learns that she must rely on her own strength and self-confidence to overcome her fears about the scary old tree in her front yard and performing a flying side kick. While this book does promote the art of Tae Kwan Do as a way of building confidence, it also explores alternative notions about courage. The illustrations and text also present positive images about gender expectations for girls and women.

Rathman, Peggy. *Ruby the Copycat*. New York: Scholastic, 1991.
ISBN#0-59043-747X GR K-1 (P) [Problem-Solving Teasing & Bullying]
Ruby is new to school and unsure how to fit in. When she insists on copying Angela, the most popular girl in class — from top to toe — she learns that sometimes it's hard to learn to be yourself. This book looks at a kind of teasing particularly common (and annoying) in the early grades and provides an opportunity to talk about how it feels as well as how to cope.

Robinson, Nancy K. *Wendy and the Bullies*. New York: Scholastic, 1983.
ISBN# 0-5903-2975-8 GR 2-3 (C) [Problem-Solving Teasing & Bullying]
Wendy knows where all the bullies are, but what can she do about them — especially when she's face to face with a dangerous bully like Stanley Kane? Wendy's troubles with bullies, both in and out of school, make her afraid to go to school.

Rosner, Ruth. *I Hate My Best Friend*. New York: Hyperion Books for Children, 1997.
ISBN# 0-786811-692 GR 2-3 (ER/C) [Problem-Solving Teasing & Bullying; Friendship]
Nini and Annie are inseparable best friends until, one day, Nini begins to put her friend down, teases and embarrasses her in front of others, and excludes her from activities they normally do together. Things escalate when Nini's cousin Irina arrives from Russia. This book provides opportunities to talk about how changes in alliances happen in friendships and how that feels, and also addresses exclusion and other types of teasing.

Scieszka, Jon. *The True Story of the Three Pigs by A. Wolf*. New York: Puffin Books, 1996.
ISBN# 0-1405-4451-8 GR 1-4 (P/ER) [Barriers; Problem-Solving Teasing & Bullying]
This humorous rewrite of the popular fairy tale tells the story of the (nasty, bullying) three pigs from the point of view of the (victimized and peace-loving) wolf. It provides an opportunity to talk about how prejudice and preconceived ideas about others can influence our

KEY: (P) = picture book (ER) = easy reader (C) =chapter book (V) = video
GR = approximate grade level [Courage; Barriers] = themes, lessons, issues

opinions and also to discuss non-violent solutions to conflicts.

Seuss, Dr. *The Sneetches.* New York: Random House, 1961.
ISBN# 0-394800-893   GR 1-3+ (P/ER) [Perspective-Taking; Barriers; Problem-Solving]
   This book contains a variety of stories which can be used to discuss conflicts, including "The Zax," about two creatures who "stick to their guns" and literally refuse to budge an inch to resolve their dilemma. This story provides opportunities for students to brainstorm solutions, to evaluate whether solutions might be effective, and to explore the notion of how "give and take" can be used, too.

Seuss, Dr. *The Butter Battle.* New York: Random House, 1984.
ISBN# 0-394865-804   GR 1-3 (P) [Rules; Problem-Solving]
   Two nations dispute over the proper way to eat buttered bread. In the process, they keep building bigger weapons. This book raises opportunities to talk about how rules are made, and what happens if rules are broken or ignored.

Shreve, Susan. *Joshua T. Bates Takes Charge.* New York: Knopf, 1993.
ISBN#0-394-84362-2   GR 3 (C)   [Problem-Solving Teasing & Bullying; Courage; Peer Pressure]
   Just as 11-year-old Joshua is beginning to recover from the humiliating experience of being held back (well, almost) after third grade, he finds himself paired with a new kid, who is the brunt of teasing by their classmates, and the target of a fifth grade bully. This is a realistic story about how a typical boy struggles to fit in, deals with peer pressure, and stands up for what he knows is right. It provides a terrific perspective from a bystander's point of view, with good examples of gender-based teasing and put-downs like "sissy" and "nerd."
It provides opportunities to talk about the courage it takes to respond to teasing and bullying, and how adults' behavior can facilitate bullying.

Silverstein, Shel. *Where the Sidewalk Ends.* New York: Harper & Row, 1970.
ISBN# 0-0602-5667-2   GR K-3 (ER) [Rules; Perspective-Taking]
   Many poems in this book, including "Us," "Sarah Cynthia Sylvia Stout Wouldn't Take the Garbage Out," and "I'm Making A List," provide opportunities to discuss rules and perspective taking.

Singer, Marilyn, ed. "Sophie." *All We Need To Say: Poems about School from Tanya and Sophie.* New York: Atheneum Books for Young Readers, 1996.
ISBN# 0-6898-0667-1   GR 3-5 (ER) [Problem-Solving Teasing & Bullying]
   This brief poem talks about the differences between what teachers say and what kids experience and introduces the idea that there are some differences that make it hard to eat lunch together or play in the school yard together. Use this as a springboard for talking about differences and how they influence students' ability to get along with each other.

Surat, Michelle Maria. *Angel Child, Dragon Child.* New York: Scholastic, 1983.
ISBN# 0-590422-715   GR 1-3 (P/ER) [Barriers; Problem-Solving Teasing & Bullying]
   Ut, who has just come to the United States from Viet Nam, is teased by children in her school and picked on by a bully named Raymond. Eventually, Ut is able to resolve her problems and to her surprise befriends the bully. This book provides opportunities to talk about teasing and how it feels, the role that bystanders have, and perspective-taking — about what it's like to be "the new kid" and different. Though it may be unrealistic to expect the

victim to befriend the bully, this book raises the ideas of face saving and peace offerings as strategies for resolving conflicts.

Swope, Sam. *Araboolies of Liberty Street*. New York: Potter; Distributed by Crown, 1989. ISBN# 0-51756-9604 GR 2-3 (P/ER) [Barriers]
   Fantasy/fable of a family who look and act differently and are shunned by their neighbors because they refuse to fit in. The neighborhood kids join forces to help the Araboolies when mean General Pinch orders them to move because they look different.

Udry, Janice May. *Let's be Enemies*. New York: HarperCollins Publishers, 1961. ISBN# 0-060261-307   GR K-2 (P) [Problem-Solving; Friendship]
   This is the story of two friends who have conflicts. When John decides he is fed up with his friend James' bossy ways, he declares they are enemies. This story provides opportunities to talk about how to recognize conflicts, the feelings they generate, and how they resolve conflicts with friends.

Van Allsburg, Chris. *Jumanji*. Boston: Houghton Mifflin, 1981. ISBN# 0-395-30448-2   GR 1-3 (P) [Rules]
   This well-known story is about a boy and girl who discover a mysterious game where rules defy common sense. This book brings up opportunities to talk about why rules are important, and how chaos and danger can erupt when you don't know what the rules are. It also provides a starting point to get into social problem-solving ("what if...") games.

Vigna, Judith. *Black Like Kyra, White Like Me*. Morton Grove, IL: Albert Whitman & Company, 1992. ISBN# 0-8075-0778-4   GR K-2 (P) [Barriers]
   Christy, who is white, and Kyra, who is black, are best friends at gymnastics class. When Kyra and her parents move into Christy's neighborhood, the neighbors are not friendly and openly show their prejudice. Ultimately, one white family moves away, but Kyra's family perseveres despite several acts of vandalism to their home and car. Kyra and Christy remain best friends throughout.

Viorst, Judith. *Alexander and the Terrible, Horrible, No Good, Very Bad Day*. New York: Scholastic, 1989. ISBN# 0-59042-1441   GR K-1 (P) [Feelings; Rules]
   On a day when everything goes wrong for him, Alexander is consoled by the thought that other people have bad days, too. This book provides opportunities to talk about how angry feelings can spill over and effect your day, and to problem-solve non-aggressive ways of expressing and managing them.

Waber, Bernard. *Ira Sleeps Over*. Boston: Houghton Mifflin, 1972. ISBN# 0-395-20503-4   GR K-1 (P) [Problem-Solving Teasing & Bullying]
   Ira is excited about the idea of spending the night at his friend's house until his sister teases him about how he'll get along without his teddy bear. In addition, Ira now worries that his friend will tease him, too. This book provides opportunities to talk about peer pressure, and how even the fear of being teased can ruin your day.

KEY: (P) = picture book (ER) = easy reader (C) =chapter book (V) = video
GR = approximate grade level [Courage; Barriers] = themes, lessons, issues

Webster-Doyle, Terrence. *Why Is Everybody Always Picking on Me?: A Guide to Handle Bullies*. Middlebury, VT: Atrium Society Publications, 1991.
ISBN# 0-94294-122-5   GR 3+ (C) [Problem-Solving Teasing & Bullying]
   This self-help book includes stories and activities that demonstrate how to resolve conflicts nonviolently and how to use self-defense techniques to peacefully confront hostile aggression. Because it is geared to older students, it is included in this section so that parents and teachers can decide whether all or part of this book might be appropriate for their children or students.

White, E.B. *Charlotte's Web*. New York: Dell, 1952.
ISBN# 0-440011-780   GR 2-3 (C) [Problem-Solving Teasing & Bullying; Courage]
   When Wilbur goes to live on a new farm, away from his friend Fern, he is lonely and forlorn. Teased by the various barnyard creatures, he is finally befriended by Charlotte, a wise and plucky spider. This book can be read aloud to second graders. It provides numerous opportunities to talk about teasing and bullying behavior, being different, and how courage and perseverance can help you overcome obstacles.

Wondriska, William. *All the Animals Were Angry*. New York: Holt, Rinehart and Winston, 1970. ISBN# 0-0308-5120-3   GR K-1 (P) [Barriers]
   All the animals criticize each other because of their differences, and this provides an opportunity to talk about barriers to getting along.

Yashima, Taro. *Crow Boy*. New York: Puffin/Penguin Books, 1976. ISBN#0-14-050172-x
GR 2-3 (P) [Barriers; Perspective-Taking; Problem-Solving Teasing & Bullying]
   Set in a small Japanese village, this book tells the story of an isolated child called Chibi, who is taunted by his peers and is made out to be the class clown. He is ignored by his bewildered teachers until the sixth grade, when his sensitive male teacher takes the time to find out about this boy and his special talent. When he displays a remarkable talent, he is given a new nickname, Crow Boy. This Caldecott Honor Book provides opportunities to discuss a variety of issues, including the hurtful effects of teasing and bullying, and roles that adults can have in setting a tone for teasing and bullying to take place. While this book can be read to even younger children, better discussions are achieved in grades 2 or over.

Zolotow, Charlotte. *The Hating Book*. New York: Harper & Row, 1989.
ISBN# 0-64431-975 GR K-2 (P) [Friendship; Perspective-Taking]
   After a series of slights cause a falling out between two friends, one girl gathers the courage to ask her friend why she is being so mean, only to discover that there is another point of view on this problem. This book provides opportunities to practice taking another person's point of view. For older students, it also provides a starting point to talk about whether adult advice is helpful and to discuss what kinds of help and support they'd like from adults when they are confronted by bullying problems.

Zolotow, Charlotte. *The Quarreling Book*. New York: Harper & Row, 1981.
ISBN# 0-64430-346 GR K-2 (P) [Problem-Solving]
   A negative chain reaction begins in the James family when Mr. James forgets to kiss Mrs.

James, who vents her frustration on her son, Jonathan. Before long, little Eddie pushes the dog, who begins a positive reaction.

Zolotow, Charlotte. *William's Doll*. New York: HarperCollins, 1972.
ISBN#0-06-02-7047-0 GR K-2 (P) [Problem-Solving Teasing & Bullying; Barriers; Courage]
   William wants a doll, but he is teased by his friends, and even some members of his family don't understand why. The grandmother explains her reasons for buying William the doll he wants, giving a moving account of the importance of developing gentle, caring, nurturing behavior. This book provides opportunities to talk about gender stereotypes and the teasing that can result, and also the way adult opinions can affect kid's attitudes and behaviors.

AUDIO VISUALS
(Please note: Many of the books listed above may also be available on audio tapes.)

And the Children Shall Lead. A Rainbow Television Workshop Production.
Salt Lake City, Utah: BWE Video, 1996. GR 3-5 (V) [Barriers; Courage]
   Set in 1964 in Catesville, Mississippi during civil rights movement struggles to get blacks to register to vote amidst daunting retaliation by whites and the Ku Klux Klan. A group of 12 year-olds help adults overcome racial barriers.

Everyone Gets Scared Sometimes and I Get So Mad! Pleasantville, NY: Sunburst Communications, 1993. GR K-2 (V) [Courage]
   This two-part video makes children aware that everyone feels scared sometimes and explains how fear can be controlled — and also keep them safe; it helps them cope with anger constructively.

Molly's Pilgrim. New York: Phoenix/BFA Films and Videos. Produced by Jeff Brown and Chris Pelzer, 1985. GR 2-4 (V) [Barriers; Teasing & Bullying]
   Based on the book by Barbara Cohen, this poignant film is set in the present day and vividly captures Molly's experiences of being bullied by her classmates for being different, as well as her own discomfort as she struggles to be like her peers.

My Friends and Me. Pleasantville, NY: Sunburst Communications, 1992.
GR K-2 (V) [Friendship; Barriers]
   This video focuses on how to make friends and how to keep them.

The Point. Nilsson House Music Inc., Murakami Wolf Productions Inc. Directed and animated by Fred Wolf, 1986. GR 3+ (V) [Bullying; Diversity]
   Based on Harry Nilsson's original tale, this is the story of a little boy named Oblio, who is born with a round shaped head among a society of people with pointed heads. Follow Oblio through his adventures in exile as he meets many other creatures who tell him how special he is to be different. (Ends happily ever after — Oblio comes home, he's accepted, and everyone else gets a rounded head.)

KEY: (P) = picture book (ER) = easy reader (C) =chapter book   (V) = video
GR = approximate grade level [Courage; Barriers] = themes, lessons, issues

A Rainbow of Feelings and Wonderful Me. Pleasantville, NY: Sunburst Communications, 1993. GR K-2 (V) [Feelings; Courage]

This two-part video introduces children to the range of human feelings, helps them realize that these are part of life, and makes the point that children's feelings about themselves (self esteem) affect how willing they are to take risks.

Stress Busters and All About Anger. Pleasantville, NY: Sunburst Communications, 1991. GR 1-4 (V) [Feelings; Anger Management & Stress Reduction]

This two-part video explains what stress is, provides simple techniques children can use to cope, and makes them aware that, while the feelings anger produces may not always be within their control, how they act on them is.

POSTERS

Be a Buddy Not a Bully (poster). Mid-Atlantic Equity Consortium, Inc., 5454 Wisconsin Ave., Chevy Case, MD 20815.

Problem Solving Without Fights (McGruff poster). Available from the National Crime Prevention Council. See their web-site on the internet for ordering information.

TOOLS FOR TEACHERS AND PARENTS

The following books are included in this section because they can provide useful information for adults and, with guidance, can be used selectively with children.

Berry, Joy. *Let's Talk About Being Bullied.* Chicago: Children's Press. 1986.
ISBN# 0-51602-695-x GR K-1 [Problem-Solving Teasing & Bullying]
This book, part of the "Let's Talk About" problem-solving series, is designed for parents to use with children as a springboard to talking about being bullied or being a bully. It is somewhat didactic, but may be useful with a particular child in mind.

Cohen-Posey, Kate. *How to Handle Bullies, Teasers and Other Meanies: A Book That Takes the Nuisance Out of Name-Calling and Other Nonsense.* Highland City, FL: Rainbow Books, 1995.
ISBN# 1-56825-029-0 GR 3+ [Problem-Solving Teasing & Bullying]
This self-help book for children provides information on why children tease and bully others and how to handle them. It also addresses prejudice and provides some self-defense tips. Because this book is written for older students, we have included it in this section so that parents and teachers can decide whether all or part of this book might be appropriate for their children or students.

Goedecke, Christopher J. *Smart Moves: A Kid's Guide to Self-Defense.* New York: Simon and Schuster Books for Young Readers, 1995.
ISBN# 0-68980-294-3 GR 3+ [Problem-Solving Teasing & Bullying]
This self-help book for students uses photographs by Rosemarie Hausherr to illustrate self-defense strategies as a way of responding to bullying. Though it is written for students, it is included in this section so that parents and teachers can decide whether all or part of this book might be appropriate for their children or students, and whether this is a strategy they feel might be useful to promote.

Hammerseng, Kathryn M. *Telling Isn't Tattling.* Seattle: Parenting Press, 1995. ISBN# 1-884734-06-5 GR 2-3 [Problem-Solving Teasing & Bullying]
A book that helps children learn to differentiate between telling an adult when intervention is needed and tattling on a friend when no one is being harmed. Provides situations and offers several actions children can choose to take.

Humphrey, Sara McLeod. *If You Had To Choose, What Would You Do?* Amherst, NY: Prometheus Books, 1995. ISBN# 1-5733392-010-x.
These 25 problem situations presented as short story-vignettes encourage students to think about what they would do in various social situations and why. Several focus on issues of teasing, exclusion, bullying, and peer pressure and are suitable supplements for elementary-age students.

Johnston, Marianne. *Dealing with Bullying.* New York: PowerKids Press, 1996. ISBN# 0-82392-374-6 GR 3+ [Problem-Solving Teasing & Bullying]
This self-help book for students describes what is meant by bullying, why bullies act the way they do, how to deal with them, and how to stop acting like a bully.

Kreidler, William. *Teaching Conflict Resolution through Children's Literature in Preschool through Grade 2.* New York: Scholastic Professional Books, 1994. ISBN# 0-590-49747-2
Provides a variety of conflict resolution activities linked to age-appropriate literature.

Lucas, Eileen. *Peace on the Playground: Non-Violent Ways of Problem-Solving.* New York: Franklin Watts, 1991. ISBN# 0-531-20047-7
A book that discusses peaceful solutions to problems in the larger world and in the daily lives of children. Addresses nonviolent problem-solving, cooperative play, and how to work toward breaking down barriers between people.

Romain, Trevor. *Bullies Are a Pain in the Brain.* Minneapolis, MN: Free Spirit Press, 1997. ISBN# 1-57542-02306 GR 3+ [Problem-Solving Teasing & Bullying]
This serious yet humorous self-help book is written for kids who are bullied, as well as those who do the bullying. It includes myths and facts about bullies, as well as strategies to get help or stand up to a bully. Because this book is written for older students, we have included it in this section so that parents and teachers can decide whether all or part of this book might be appropriate for their children or students.

Stein, Nan and Sjostrom, Lisa. *Bullyproof: A Teacher's Guide on Teasing and Bullying for Use With Fourth and Fifth Grade Students.* A joint publication of Wellesley College Center for Research on Women, Wellesley, MA and NEA Professional Library, Washington, D.C., 1996. ISBN# 0-96412-211-x
Eleven sequential core lessons comprised of writing activities, reading assignments, class discussions, role-plays, case studies, and homework assignments that help students focus on the boundaries between appropriate and inappropriate behavior.

KEY: (P) = picture book (ER) = easy reader (C) =chapter book (V) = video
GR = approximate grade level [Courage; Barriers] = themes, lessons, issues

Stewart, Mary and Kathy Phillips. *Yoga for Children*. New York: Simon & Schuster Inc. (A Fireside Book), 1992. ISBN# 0-671-78712-8

  Children from diverse racial and ethnic groups demonstrate simple yoga exercises that promote flexibility, stress reduction, relaxation, and coordination.

RESOURCES FOR TEACHERS AND PARENTS

Bullard, Sara. *Teaching Tolerance: Raising Open-minded Empathetic Children*. New York: Doubleday, 1996. ISBN# 0-3854-7264-1

Cecil, Nancy Lee with Patricia L. Roberts. *Raising Peaceful Children in a Violent World*. San Diego: Lura Media, Inc., 1995. ISBN# 1-880913-16-X

Cohn, Janice. *Raising Compassionate Caring Children in a Violent World*. Atlanta, GA: Longstreet Press, 1996. ISBN# 1-56352-276-4

Fried, SuEllen and Paula Fried. *Bullies and Victims: Helping Your Child through the Schoolyard Battlefield*. New York: M. Evans & Co., Inc., 1996. ISBN# 0-87131-807-5

Levin, Diane E. *Teaching Young Children in Violent Times: Building a Peaceable Classroom*. Cambridge, MA: Educators for Social Responsibility, 1994. ISBN# 0-86571-316-2

Olweus, Dan. *Bullying in Schools: What We Know and What We Can Do*. Cambridge, MA: Blackwell Publishers, Inc., 1993. ISBN# 0-631-19241-7

Paley, Vivian Gussin. *You Can't Say You Can't Play*. Cambridge, MA: Harvard University Press, 1992. ISBN# 0-674-96589-2

Ross, Dorothea. *Childhood Teasing and Bullying: What School Personnel, Other Professionals and Parents Can Do*. Alexandria, VA: American Counseling Association, 1996. ISBN# 1-55620-157-5

Slaby, Ronald, Wendy Roedell, Diana Arezzo, and Kate Hendrix. *Early Violence Prevention: Tools for Teachers of Young Children*. Washington, D.C.: National Association for the Education of Young Children, 1995. ISBN# 0-935989-65-X

Stein, Nan. *Bullying and Sexual Harassment in Elementary Schools: It's Not Just Kids Kissing Kids*. Working Paper #284. Wellesley, MA: Wellesley College Center for Research on Women, 1997.

Train, Alan. *The Bullying Problem: How to Deal with Difficult Children*. London: Human Horizons/Souvenir Press, 1995. ISBN# 0285632558

INTERNET RESOURCES

Bullying and Victimization in Schools listserv: Send e-mail to "NET::Listserv@nic.surfnet.nl"
   In the message portion of your e-mail, type in your first and last name; you will then receive further instructions about how to proceed.

Kidscape: http://www.solnet.co.uk/kidscape/kids4.htm
   This British-based site has lots of interesting information about bullying for adults and students, including guides called *You Can Beat Bullying — A Guide for Young People*, and *Preventing Bullying — A Parent's Guide*.

National Crime Prevention Council: http://www.ncpc.org
   This site has resources and articles on teasing and bullying.

National Organizations of Parent Teacher Associations: http://www.pto.org/programs
   This site has resources and articles on teasing and bullying.

Sesame Street Parents/Children's Television Workshop: http://www.ctw.org/parents/weekly
   This site has articles on gender, aggression, and teasing and bullying and links to other sites. Articles report separately for three age groups: birth to two, two to five, and six to eleven years.

KEY: (P) = picture book (ER) = easy reader (C) =chapter book (V) = video
GR = approximate grade level [Courage; Barriers] = themes, lessons, issues

Appendix I: REFERENCES: FOR FURTHER READING

Ahmad, Y., & Smith, P.K. (1994). Bullying in schools and the issue of sex differences. In J. Archer (Ed.), *Male violence.* London: Routledge.

Andersen, M.L. (1993). *Thinking about women: Sociological perspectives on sex and gender: Third edition.* New York: Macmillan Publishing Company.

Bjorkqvist, K. (1994). Sex differences in physical, verbal, and indirect aggression: A review of recent research. *Sex Roles: A Journal of Research*, 30 (3-4), 177-188.

Charach, A., Pepler, D., & Ziegler, S. (1995). Bullying at school: A Canadian perspective. *Education Canada, Spring/Printemps*, 13-18.

Corbett, K., Gentry, C.S., & Pearson, W. (1993). Sexual harassment in high school. *Youth & Society*, 25 (1), 93-103.

Hazler, R.J., Hoover, J.H., & Oliver, R. (1991). Student perceptions of victimization by bullies in school. *Journal of Humanistic Education and Development*, 29, 143-150.

Hoover, J.H., Oliver, R.L., & Thomson, K.A. (1993). Perceived victimization by school bullies: New research and future research. *Journal of Humanistic Education and Development*, 32, 76-84.

Kohlberg, L. (1966). A cognitive-developmental analysis of children's sex-role concepts and attitudes. In E. Maccoby (Ed.), *The development of sex differences.* Stanford, CA: Stanford University Press, 82-166.

Maccoby, E.E. & Jacklin, C.N. (1974). *The psychology of sex differences.* Stanford, CA: Stanford University Press.

Mooney, A., Creeser, R., & Blatchford, P. (1991). Children's views on teasing and fighting in junior schools. *Educational Research*, 33 (2), 103-112.

Olweus, D. (1993). *Bullying at school: What we know and what we can do.* Oxford, UK: Blackwell.

Olweus, D. (1994). Annotation: Bullying at school: Basic facts and effects of a school based intervention program. *Journal of Child Psychology & Psychiatry*, 35 (7), 1171-1190.

Parke, R.D., & Slaby, R.G. (1983). The development of aggression. In P.H. Mussen (Series Ed.) & E.M. Hetherington (Volume Ed.), *Handbook of Child Psychology: Vol. 4. Socialization, personality, and social development* (pp. 547-641). New York: Wiley.

Richardson, L. (1988). *The dynamics of sex and gender: A sociological perspective: Third edition.* New York: Harper & Row, Publishers.

Rigby, K., & Slee, P.T. (1991). Bullying among Australian school children: Reported behavior and attitudes toward victims. *The Journal of Social Psychology*, 131 (5), 615-627.

Ross, D.M. (1996). *Childhood bullying and teasing: What school personnel, other professionals, and parents can do.* Alexandria, VA: American Counseling Association.

Saegert, S., & Hart, R. (1978). The development of environmental competence in girls and boys. In M. Salter (Ed.), *Play: An anthropological perspective*. West Point, NY: Leisure Press.

Smith, P.K., & Thompson, D. (1991). Dealing with bully/victim problems in the U.K. In P.K. Smith & D. Thompson (Eds.), *Practical approaches to bullying* (pp. 1-12). London: Fulton.

Stein, N. (1995). Sexual harassment in school: The public performance of gendered violence. *Harvard Educational Review* (65) 2, 145-162.

Stephenson, P., & Smith, D. (1989). Bullying in the junior school. In D.P. Tattum & D.A. Lane (Eds.), *Bullying in schools* (pp. 45-57). Hanley, Stoke-on-Trent: Trentham Books.

Tattum, D.P. (1989). Violence and aggression in schools. In D.P. Tattum & D.A. Lane (Eds.), *Bullying in schools* (pp. 7-19). Hanley, Stoke-on-Trent: Trentham Books.

Thorne, B. (1994). *Gender play: Girls and boys in school*. New Brunswick, NJ: Rutgers University Press.

Thorne, B. & Luria, Z. (1986). Sexuality and gender in children's daily worlds. *Social Problems*, 33, 3, pp.176-190.

Unger, R. & Crawford, M. (1992). *Women and gender: A feminist psychology*. New York: McGraw-Hill, Inc.

Whitney, I., & Smith, P.K. (1993). A survey of the nature and extent of bullying in junior/middle and secondary schools. *Educational Research*, 35 (1), 3-25.

Appendix II: HISTORY OF THE PROJECT: GENDER-BASED TEASING AND BULLYING IN GRADES K-5

BACKGROUND

This Guide grew out of a series of collegial discussions between Educational Equity Concepts (EEC) and the Wellesley College Center for Research on Women (WCCRW) that began in 1993. Both organizations were concerned about the nature and amount of teasing and bullying, much of it gender-based, occurring in elementary schools across the country. More and more frequently, we were hearing reports about behavior such as "flip days," in which boys were "officially" allowed to pull up girls' skirts; about boys insulting girls who were developing breasts by mooing at them; about girls being called derogatory terms like "ho" (meaning whore). It was also around this time that we read about Cheltzie Hentz, the seven-year-old who had to ride to her school in Eden Prairie, Minnesota, on a bus with boys who called her "bitch" and a driver who seemed to think it was funny. As a result, Cheltzie's mother filed a complaint with the state Department of Human Rights and with the U.S. Education Department's Office for Civil Rights, which led to the April 1993 U.S. Education Department ruling that the Eden Prairie Schools had violated federal law by "failing to take timely and effective responsive action."

Dr. Nan Stein, a Senior Researcher at WCCRW who had conducted extensive research into peer-to-peer sexual harassment in high school, already had begun to look at such behavior in grades 4-5, framing it in the context of bullying at this grade level. This research eventually led to the publication of *Bullyproof: A Teacher's Guide on Teasing and Bullying for Use with Fourth and Fifth Grade Students.* EEC, which had a long history of working on gender issues in early childhood education, was interested in conducting research and developing a companion guide for the K-3 level. Thus, a collaboration between the two organizations was born.

In 1995, EEC was awarded a two-year grant from the U.S. Department of Education's Women's Educational Equity Act (WEEA) to collaborate with WCCRW to conduct "Gender-Based Teasing and Bullying in Grades K-5," a research and curriculum development project. In the second year of the grant, funding was shifted to the U.S. Department of Education's Safe and Drug Free Schools and Communities Act program, which funds a broad range of anti-violence projects. Clearly, the Department of Education understood the importance of addressing teasing and bullying behavior at the earliest level of education as a deterrent to violence in schools at the upper levels.

In this Guide, classroom lessons and activities are targeted to grades K-3. This Guide, along with *Bullyproof* for grades 4-5, offers schools a comprehensive approach to addressing teasing and bullying behavior at the elementary level.

RESEARCH

Dr. Nancy Gropper, Associate Professor of Elementary Education at SUNY/New Paltz, joined the project in the role of Research/Evaluator. In this role, she designed the research methodology, trained the classroom observers, and analyzed the results. Prior to the beginning of the project, a research protocol was developed with seed grants from two New York City foundations. Classroom visits were conducted in a New York City public school to observe how teasing and bullying manifested itself in the early grades. So when full funding was achieved in 1995, the protocol was ready, and the research phase of the project commenced.

Our research on teasing and bullying was conducted in racially, culturally, and economically diverse public schools in New York City and Framingham, Massachusetts. A diverse team of research assistants was hired and trained in both locations to carry out the study, which included: 1) Classroom observations in grades K-3; 2) Interviews with students from those same K-3 classrooms; 3) Focus groups with teachers from K-3 classrooms; and 4) Focus groups with parents across grades K-5.

The data from 25 K-3 classrooms showed that gender is a subtle but relevant factor in incidents of teasing and bullying. In most cases, it is the gender of the participants and how the incident is perceived, rather than the content itself, that is significant.

Seventy-eight percent of the 321 observed incidents were initiated by boys, although boys and girls were equally likely to be recipients or bystanders regardless of the gender of the initiator(s). A small number of gender-explicit or sexual incidents occurred (26), 80% of which were initiated by boys, but with boys and girls equally likely to be the recipients of such incidents. The fact that both girls and boys are bullied more by boys is in keeping with the research on bullying conducted by researchers in Europe, Canada, and the United States.

Teachers and other adults in the classroom were uninvolved in or ignored a large majority (71%) of the observed incidents. Dr. Dan Olweus, who has researched bullying for more than 20 years, also has found that students report that teachers do relatively little to put a stop to bullying behavior.[1]

When interviewed, a sample of boys from the classrooms in which the observations occurred described incidents in which 95% of the initiators were boys and 91% of the recipients were also boys. The sample of girls who were interviewed described incidents in which only 54% of the initiators were boys but 76% of the recipients were girls. The majority of boys (81%) and girls (62%) believed that teachers were looking when these incidents occurred. They uniformly expressed the desire that teachers intervene rather than ignore teasing and bullying situations.

The focus group meetings indicated that both teachers and parents are very aware of and concerned about bullying and teasing. Teachers reported that among K-3 students any observable difference can be a trigger for teasing and bullying; that it has an impact on their ability to teach; that there is a need for consistent school policies to address such incidents; and that early intervention is important. Parents were concerned with how to help their children deal with teasing and bullying, particularly when a verbal response does not stop the initiator. They were concerned about what to do when school policies conflict with their beliefs about how to address this issue.

DEVELOPMENT OF THE GUIDE

The research conducted by EEC and WCCRW in New York City and Framingham, Massachusetts, underscored by the existing base of research on teasing and bullying behavior, formed the foundation of this Guide. In addition to our observations during all parts of the school day, interviews with students and focus groups with teachers and parents provided invaluable information that shaped the lessons and activities herein.

The Guide underwent pilot testing in New York City and Newton, Massachusetts in a total of 15 classrooms. The teachers and students who participated represented a diverse group, racially, ethnically, and economically. Teachers were asked to try out the activities as written, and to provide critical feedback through written forms, individual interviews, and group meetings. Teachers were also encouraged to adapt the activities to meet the needs of their particular students and to develop extensions of their own. The pilot teachers did all of that and more. They provided samples of student's work, shared worksheets they had developed, suggested resource materials, and noted wonderful anecdotes about students' verbatim responses to the activities.

As part of the pilot process, we also visited classrooms to observe activities as they were being tried and met with the teachers to discuss their experiences and to receive face-to-face feedback. A few weeks after pilot testing was completed, telephone interviews were conducted by the outside evaluator with many of the teachers to obtain additional information about their perceptions about the impact of the lessons and activities on students' behavior. Ideas and insights generated by teachers and students have been incorporated throughout the Guide.

---

[1] D. Olweus, *Bullying at School: What We Know and What We Can Do* (Oxford, UK: Blackwell, 1993).

Appendix III: ABOUT THE CONTRIBUTORS

Authors

MERLE FROSCHL, CO-FOUNDER AND CO-DIRECTOR OF EDUCATIONAL EQUITY CONCEPTS, served as Project Director for "Gender-Based Teasing and Bullying in Grades K-5." Currently, she is Co-Principal Investigator of Playtime is Science for Children with Disabilities and Creating Afterschool Opportunities for Girls in New York City Settlement Houses.

Ms. Froschl has 35 years of experience in education and publishing. Since the 1970s she has developed outstanding curricular and teacher training models in the field of educational equity. Ms. Froschl was national Field-Testing Director of the Women's Lives/Women's Work Series for high school English and Social Studies teachers at the Feminist Press, where she developed one of the first inservice courses on nonsexist education for teachers in grades K-12. She is a nationally-known speaker on issues of gender equity and equality of opportunity in education, co-chair of the Early Childhood Task Force of the National Coalition for Sex Equity in Education, and a long-standing member of the Sex Equity Task Force for the New York City Board of Education.

Merle Froschl has authored and edited a number of articles, teacher's guides, and books including *Evaluating Curricular Materials for Bias: Guidelines for the Review of Instructional Materials* (New York City Board of Education); *Resources for Educational Equity* (Garland Publishing); *What Will Happen If... Young Children and the Scientific Method, Playtime is Science: An Equity-Based Parent/Child Science Program,* and *Including All Of Us: An Early Childhood Curriculum About Disability* (Educational Equity Concepts). Most recently, in addition to this Guide, Ms. Froschl was the editor for *Bridging the Gap: A National Directory of Services for Women and Girls with Disabilities* (Educational Equity Concepts, second edition). Merle Froschl holds a B.S. in Journalism from Syracuse University and is a graduate of the Institute for Not-for-Profit Management, Columbia University.

Authors (con't)

BARBARA SPRUNG, CO-FOUNDER AND CO-DIRECTOR OF EDUCATIONAL EQUITY CONCEPTS, served as Research Director for "Gender-Based Teasing and Bullying in Grades K-5." She currently is Co-Principal Investigator of Playtime is Science for Children with Disabilities and Creating Afterschool Opportunities for Girls in New York City Settlement Houses.

Ms. Sprung has 40 years of experience in the field of early childhood education, as a classroom teacher, curriculum and program developer, and teacher trainer. She was the founder and Director of the Non-Sexist Child Development Project at the Women's Action Alliance where she pioneered in the development of the first non-sexist, multiracial, and "inclusionary" teaching materials, toys, and audiovisual classroom aids.

Barbara Sprung has written many articles on early sex-role development and has authored and edited books including *Non-Sexist Education for Young Children: A Practical Guide* (Citation Press, Scholastic); *Perspectives on Non-Sexist Early Childhood Education* (Teachers College Press); *Resources for Educational Equity*, (Garland Publishing); *What Will Happen If... Young Children and the Scientific Method* and *Playtime is Science* (Educational Equity Concepts); and *Learning About Family Life* (Rutgers University Press). Most recently, in addition to this Guide, she has authored two books in a series for preteens, *Preteen Pressures: Stress* and *Preteen Pressures: Death* (Raintree Steck-Vaughn) and the K-1 segment of *Our Whole Lives (O.W.L)* curriculum, part of a series to be published by the Universalist Unitarian Association. Barbara Sprung holds a B.A. in Early Childhood Education from Sarah Lawrence College, an M.S. in Child Development from the Bank Street College of Education, and is a graduate of the Institute for Not-for-Profit Management, Columbia University.

Authors (con't)

NANCY MULLIN-RINDLER, RESEARCH ASSOCIATE AT THE CENTER FOR RESEARCH ON WOMEN AT WELLESLEY COLLEGE, served as Massachusetts Site Coordinator of "Gender-Based Teasing and Bullying in Grades K-5." She currently is Associate Director of the Project on Teasing and Bullying.

Ms. Mullin-Rindler has 25 years of experience in the fields of elementary, early childhood, and special education as a teacher, trainer, consultant, and advocate. She regularly conducts teacher training and parent seminars on teasing and bullying across the country, including the Wellesley College Center for Research on Women Summer Workshops series. In addition, Ms. Mullin-Rindler is a Research Associate of the Massachusetts site of the National Institute on Child Health and Human Development Study of Early Child Care; and provides training and consultation to early childhood teachers about creating empathy in classrooms.

Nancy Mullin-Rindler has written and co-authored several training guides, as well as articles for parents and teachers on child care, resource and referral, and child development issues, including: *Teaching Children to Care: An Empathy Curriculum for Preschoolers* (in press); *TV's Youngest Viewers: Infants, Toddlers* (Wellesley College Center for Research on Women); *Child Care Resource and Referral: Counselors and Trainers Manual* (Redleaf Press/Gryphon House); and *In-Home Child Care: A Resource Guide* (Work/Family Directions). She has co-authored posters presented at the Society for Research on Child Development and the National Head Start Research Conference. Ms. Mullin-Rindler holds a B.S. in Elementary and Special Education from Slippery Rock University and an M.Ed. from the University of Pittsburgh.

Senior Consultants

NAN STEIN IS A SENIOR RESEARCH SCIENTIST AT THE CENTER FOR RESEARCH ON WOMEN AT WELLESLEY COLLEGE where she directs several national research projects on sexual harassment, gender violence, and teasing and bullying in schools. She was Co-Principal Investigator and lead author of the *Seventeen* magazine (September 1992) survey on sexual harassment in the schools, Secrets in Public: Sexual Harassment in Our Schools, and is co-author of two teaching guides, *Flirting or Hurting? A Teacher's Guide on Student-to-Student Sexual Harassment in Schools for Grades 6 through 12* (1994), and *Bullyproof: A Teacher's Guide on Teasing and Bullying for use with Fourth and Fifth Grade Students* (1996). Dr. Stein has written numerous articles for educational publications including, *Educational Leadership, Education Week, West's Education Law Reporter* and the *Harvard Educational Review*. She is a nationally-known speaker on issues of sexual harassment, appearing on many popular news and talk show programs.

Prior to joining the Center for Research on Women, Nan Stein had been working in the area of sexual harassment in schools for over 19 years. Dr. Stein holds a B.A. in History from the University of Wisconsin, a M.A.T. from Antioch College Graduate School of Education, and a Doctorate in Education from Harvard University Graduate School of Education.

Senior Consultants (con't)

NANCY GROPPER IS AN ASSISTANT PROFESSOR, SCHOOL OF EDUCATION, BROOKLYN COLLEGE, CITY UNIVERSITY OF NEW YORK. Since 1977, when she wrote her doctoral dissertation on "The Development of Sex-Typing, Gender Constancy, and Classification in Young Children," Dr. Gropper has conducted research and published articles on sex-role socialization and the implications for education in the *Harvard Educational Review*, the *Journal of Teacher Education,* and *Children Today.* Dr. Gropper has also given lectures and workshops on active learning approaches at early childhood education conferences and programs nationally and internationally and has served as an evaluation consultant for a variety of educational and research programs.

Dr. Gropper has conducted a longitudinal study on the impact of changes made to the early childhood program for the Pine Bush Central School District and is a consultant to the Newburgh School District on portfolio assessment and evaluation. In 1991, she was the recipient of the new faculty development award, New Paltz Chapter, United University Professors. Dr. Gropper holds a B.S. from the University of Delaware, and an M.A. and Ed.D in Early Childhood Education from Teachers College, Columbia University.

Collaborating Organizations

EDUCATIONAL EQUITY CONCEPTS, INC. (EEC) is a national not-for-profit organization based in New York City. Founded in 1982, the organization promotes equal educational opportunity through programs and materials that counteract bias due to sex, race/ethnicity, disability, and level of family income. EEC conducts training for administrators, teachers, and parents and provides written and hands-on materials for use in and out of the classroom. A major premise of the organization is the need to begin early to decrease discrimination. EEC has pioneered the design of equity-focused early education programs, working to sharpen public awareness of the connection between early childhood socialization practices and later adolescent/adult behavior.

WELLESLEY COLLEGE CENTER FOR RESEARCH ON WOMEN, founded in 1974, houses an interdisciplinary community of scholars who conduct cutting-edge research examining the lives of women in a changing world. All work is informed by the rich and varied perspectives of women from diverse backgrounds. Center research helps to shape public policy and promote positive social and institutional change. The Center is committed to improving the quality of life for all people. Results of Center research are reported in the Working Papers booklet as well as in Research Report, published twice a year.

1

(32)

DL { 106
    { 105 UHS

DATE DUE

IAL			
N82n			
4-25-02	WITHDRAWN		
ILL			
1069945			
8/17/05			
JY 22 '07			
JLL			
8/19/10			
GAYLORD			PRINTED IN U.S.A.